Voyager

PASSPORT READING

JOURNEYS™ III

STUDENT BOOK   PART B

PHOTO AND ART CREDITS

Expedition 8: 11, ©iStockphoto.com/Anatoly Tiplyashin; 19, ©Punchstock; 20, ©iStockphoto.com/Brue; 35, ©Courtesy of the California History Room, California State Library, Sacramento, California

Expedition 9: 43, ©Jayme Thornton/Getty Images; 57, public domain; 75, ©iStockphoto.com/Terry Wilson, ©iStockphoto.com/Sharon Dominick, ©iStockphoto.com/Mitar Holod; 76, ©iStockphoto.com/Dennis Guyitt, ©iStockphoto.com/João Lourenço, ©Wikipedia/Joelmills

Expedition 10: 78, ©iStockphoto.com/bluestocking; 103, ©iStockphoto.com/Justin Horrocks, ©iStockphoto.com/Christopher Wells, ©iStockphoto.com/Andrey Armyagov, ©iStockphoto.com/Andrey Armyagov

Expedition 11: 133, W. Robert Moore/National Geographic/Getty Images; 151, ©iStockphoto.com/Sondra Paulson, ©iStockphoto.com/Vitaliy, ©iStockphoto.com/Carolina K. Smith,M.D., ©iStockphoto.com/Andrea Gingerich, ©iStockphoto.com/Florian Loebermann; 152, ©iStockphoto.com/jean frooms

Expedition 12: 171, ©iStockphoto.com/Darko Novakovic, ©iStockphoto.com/John Peacock, ©iStockphoto.com/Victor Melniciuc, ©iStockphoto.com/Kelly Cline

Expedition 13: 197, ©Clive Rose/Getty Images; 225, ©iStockphoto.com/Dan Tero

Expanded Learning
Voyager®

ISBN 13: 978-1-4168-1614-0
ISBN: 1-4168-1614-3
210622

Printed in the United States of America   11 12 13 14 15 WEB 9 8 7 6 5
17855 Dallas Parkway, Suite 400 • Dallas, Texas 75287 • 1-888-399-1995

Table of Contents

Name _____ **Date** _____

A. Organize Your Ideas

Back in Time

- •
- •
- •

How important is it to be clean?

- •
- •
- •

Can bugs help fight infection? Explain.

- •
- •
- •

In what ways might your life today be easier than that of a teenager in the 1700s or 1800s? How might it be more difficult?

- •
- •
- •

What else would you like to know about the American past?

_____

_____

B. The Big Picture

You will read about how life was in the past. Write the big idea of each passage in the outside ovals. Connect the passages in the center oval by writing the big picture.

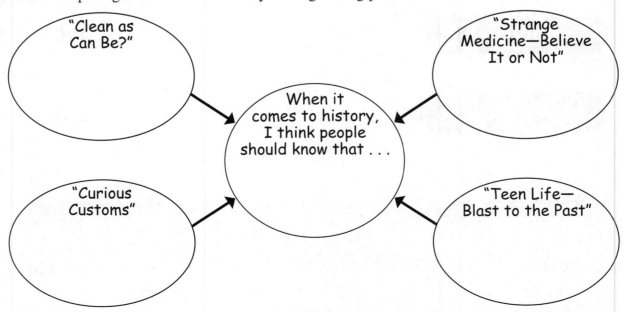

"Clean as Can Be?"

"Strange Medicine—Believe It or Not"

When it comes to history, I think people should know that . . .

"Curious Customs"

"Teen Life— Blast to the Past"

C. Expedition Dictionary

You will read the following vocabulary words throughout the Expedition. As you learn the words, use them as often as possible in your oral and written language.

"Clean as Can Be?"

rational	(adj) *reasonable and sensible*
customs	(n) *ways of doing things that have been done for a long time and are widely accepted or have become traditions*
current	(adj) *of the present time; most recent*
purpose	(n) *an aim or goal; reason for doing something*
substance	(n) *something that has weight and takes up space; matter*

"Strange Medicine—Believe It or Not"

treatment	(n) *medical method to try to cure or heal*
tolerate	(v) *put up with; bear*
prescribe	(v) *advise to take a certain medicine or treatment*
gruesome	(adj) *causing fear and disgust; horrible*
survive	(v) *stay alive through or after a dangerous event*

"Curious Customs"

contemporary	(adj) *at the present time*
qualified	(adj) *fit for a given purpose*
instruct	(v) *teach*
transaction	(n) *an exchange of goods, services, or money*
various	(adj) *of differing kinds; representing a variety*
society	(n) *people living together as a group with the same way of life*

"Teen Life—Blast to the Past"

activities	(n) *things you do*
fundamental	(adj) *basic or main; serving as the basis*
crucial	(adj) *important*
employment	(n) *a person's work; job*
social	(adj) *having to do with people coming together in a friendly group*

Dictionary Challenge

Write a story about the American past using as many of the vocabulary words as possible.

Name _____ Date _____

Vocabulary

"Clean as Can Be?"

A. Rate your knowledge of each boldfaced word.

   3   I know what this word means, and I can use it in a sentence.

   2   I have an idea of this word's meaning, but I need to know more.

   1   I don't know what this word means.

☐   **rational** (adj) *reasonable and sensible*
Soap was so hard to make in early America that it was not even *rational* to use it for bathing.

☐   **customs** (n) *ways of doing things that have been done for a long time and are widely accepted or have become traditions*
The *customs* of our ancestors seem strange because we have different ways of doing things.

☐   **current** (adj) *of the present time; most recent*
Our *current* toothpaste is much more pleasant than what people used 200 years ago.

☐   **purpose** (n) *an aim or goal; reason for doing something*
The real *purpose* of wearing wigs in the 1700s was to be fashionable.

☐   **substance** (n) *something that has weight and takes up space; matter*
Toothpaste is a sticky *substance* used to clean teeth.

B. Choose the boldfaced vocabulary word from Part A that BEST answers each of the following questions.

1. Which word goes with something that "seems to make sense"? _____

2. Which word would you use to describe the news in today's newspaper? _____

3. Which word could you use to describe glue, oil, or soap? _____

4. Which word goes with "actions that you do as a habit or at certain times of the year"?
_____

5. Which word goes with "reason for an action"? _____

C. Choose two words from Part A. Use each word in a sentence.

1. _____

     _____

2. _____

     _____

Name _____ Date _____

Word Building

A. Suffixes are word parts at the end of words. The suffix -al can mean "of" or "like" or "the act of" and is added to each of the following words. Think about the meaning of the base word to understand the word with the suffix added. Underline the base word. The first one is done for you.

<u>ration</u>al	personal	traditional	coastal

B. Sometimes more than one suffix is added. You often will notice a spelling change. Underline the base word in each of the following words. Notice the spelling changes in the suffixes.

cleanly	cleanliness	friendly	friendliness

C. Write a word from Parts A and B that BEST matches each of the following descriptions. Check that you spell each word correctly.

1. If the people in your town say hello to their neighbors, you are in this kind of town.

   _____

2. When someone is rude to you, you say they do not show this. _____

3. When a family celebrates on the holidays, they may do these kinds of things.

   _____

4. When you walk along land near the sea or ocean, you are on this type of land.

   _____

5. When you solve a problem using sensible thought, you act this way. _____

6. When you eat at a restaurant, you complain if you do not see this. _____

7. When you have an opinion about a movie, it is this kind of opinion. _____

8. When a butcher cuts a piece of meat, he cuts it this way with a sharp knife.

   _____

D. Choose two words from Parts A and B. Use each word in a sentence.

1. _____

   _____

2. _____

   _____

Name _____   Date _____

Main Idea

A. Complete the diagram using information from "Clean as Can Be?" First, write the main ideas of the paragraphs. Then, state the main idea of the passage.

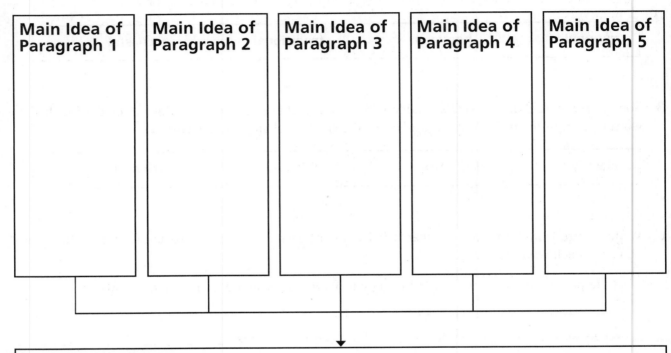

Main Idea of Paragraph 1	Main Idea of Paragraph 2	Main Idea of Paragraph 3	Main Idea of Paragraph 4	Main Idea of Paragraph 5

Main Idea of Passage

B. Write a short summary of the passage "Clean as Can Be?" Use information you wrote in the diagram.

_____

_____

_____

_____

_____

_____

_____

_____

_____

_____

_____

Name _____ Date _____

Write in Response to Reading

Imagine a teenager from one of the time periods described in "Clean as Can Be?" has been transported to the present day. This person must stay with you until he or she can get back to the past. Write a story to describe how you have tried to hide the teenager's true identity from your family and friends. Include details from the passage about hygiene that will make your story funny.

Title _____

_____

_____

_____

_____

_____

_____

_____

_____

_____

_____

_____

_____

_____

_____

_____

_____

_____

_____

_____

_____

_____

_____

_____

_____

_____

_____

Name _____   Date _____

Vocabulary

"Strange Medicine—Believe It or Not"

A. Put a check mark in each row to indicate how well you know each boldfaced word.

	Know This Word	Have Seen This Word	Don't Know This Word
treatment (n) *medical method to try to cure or heal* One *treatment* from long ago, blistering, was often worse than the illness.			
tolerate (v) *put up with; bear* I could not *tolerate* some of those painful medical practices.			
prescribe (v) *advise to take a certain medicine or treatment* People usually followed what the doctor would *prescribe* so they would get better.			
gruesome (adj) *causing fear and disgust; horrible* The medical practices during the American Civil War are too *gruesome* to talk about during lunch.			
survive (v) *stay alive through or after a dangerous event* It's amazing that some patients did *survive* the unsafe medical practices of the 1800s.			

B. Complete each sentence with the correct vocabulary word from Part A.

1. Photos showed fierce battles and other _____ scenes from different wars.

2. If you have serious allergies, your doctor may _____ medicine during hay fever season.

3. Some people do not take pain medicine because they can _____ pain better than others.

4. My grandma says the best _____ for a cold is to get a lot of sleep and eat chicken noodle soup.

5. People who take outdoor training courses are more likely to _____ if they are alone in the wilderness.

Name _____ Date _____

Word Building

A. Add word parts to build new words that have *treat* or *survive* as the base word. Be sure that the new word matches the definition. Check your work with the dictionary.

Inflectional Ending	-s	-ing		
Prefix	re-	dis-	mal-	
Suffix	-or	-ment	-al	-able

Build New Words	Definitions
treat	***give medical attention to***
1.	*able to be treated*
2.	*giving medical attention to*
3.	*medical attention given to someone*
4.	*cruel or rough treatment given to someone*
survive	***stay alive***
5.	*staying alive*
6.	*the act or process of staying alive*
7.	*one who survives*
8.	*able to survive*

B. Complete the paragraph. Use words from Part A that have *treat* or *survive* as the base word.

Many diseases were not _____ in the past. Sometimes the _____ that doctors prescribed was ineffective. Doctors and scientists didn't know enough about the diseases to _____ them successfully. After a disease infected a person, his or her chance of being a _____ was often small. Advances in medicine have made many diseases _____. You have a much better chance of _____ today. Some patients think they have received poor care if they don't get well immediately. The care people received in the past would be considered _____ today.

Name _____ Date _____

Summarize

A. Read the section summaries. Review "Strange Medicine—Believe It or Not" to identify which section each box summarizes and fill in the missing information and section headings.

Introduction

In the 18th century, doctors used methods like _____

_____, but these methods weren't often successful.

_____

Up to the late 1800s, _____,

and barbers performed this operation.

_____

Many soldiers died from _____ due to amputations.

_____

Leeches and maggots, once used to treat various ailments, are used today to _____

_____.

_____

The discovery of _____

caused doctors to use sterilization methods, and more patients survived.

B. Write a summary of the passage.

_____

_____

_____

_____

_____

_____

_____

Name _____   Date _____

Write in Response to Reading

In "Clean as Can Be?" and "Strange Medicine—Believe It or Not," you read about products used for cleaning, fashion, and medicine in the past. Choose one of these items to create an advertising campaign. Think about some of your favorite products and the billboards, radio spots, and TV commercials for them. Create a billboard for a product from the passages in the box. Below the billboard, write a radio spot or TV commercial for the product.

Billboard

Radio or TV Commercial

_____

_____

_____

_____

_____

_____

_____

_____

_____

_____

_____

Name _____   Date _____

Review Vocabulary

A. Complete each sentence with a context clue that supports the meaning of the boldfaced word. A context clue can be an example, synonym, antonym, or brief explanation. The first one is done for you.

1. Many Civil War soldiers didn't **survive**, or _____live_____, if their wound became infected.

2. In the 18th century, a doctor might **prescribe** bloodletting. He would _____ _____.

3. Our **current** bathing habits are unlike how people kept clean in the _____.

4. Years ago, doctors used leeches as a **treatment**, or _____, for disease.

5. The use of maggots was a **gruesome** method of treating wounds; it was not a _____ cure.

B. For each word in Part B, write a synonym, or a word that has the same or a similar meaning. Choose answers from the word box.

gruesome	substance	customs	rational
current	tolerate	treatment	purpose

1. reasonable _____

2. present _____

3. practice _____

4. reason _____

5. material _____

6. remedy _____

7. bear _____

8. horrible _____

C. Answer each of the following questions.

1. Describe a time when you had to **tolerate** something.

_____

_____

2. Explain the specific **purpose** for the following healthy habit.

Habit   **Purpose**

Washing your hands before eating   _____

Name _____ Date _____

Extend Vocabulary

A. The word *survive* uses the Latin root *vivere*, meaning "to live." The word *prescribe* uses the Latin root *scribere*, meaning "to write." Read the following words and their meanings. Notice how the meanings of the English words still contain the meanings of the Latin roots.

Words	Definitions	Words	Definitions
survive (v)	*stay alive through or after a dangerous event*	**prescribe** (v)	*advise to take a certain medicine or treatment*
revive (v)	*bring back to health or life*	**inscribed** (v)	*marked with letters or words on a surface*
vivid (adj)	*full of life; clear, strong (as in images)*	**describe** (v)	*tell details with words or pictures*
vivacious (adj)	*lively in temper, conduct, or spirit*	**scribble** (v)	*write or draw quickly or carelessly*

B. Think about the meanings of the words in Part A and how you have heard each word used. Choose the word that BEST completes each sentence.

1. People who are very sick are not _____.

2. The book contained _____ pictures of doctors performing operations.

3. After the car accident, the police asked us to _____ how it happened.

4. When doctors give prescriptions today, they _____ them on a pad or use a computer.

5. When people are very tired, they must get rest and drink liquids to _____ themselves.

6. Oak View Cemetery has a Civil War monument _____ with the names of soldiers from our town.

C. Choose two words from Part A. Use each word in a sentence.

1. _____

   _____

2. _____

   _____

Name _____   Date _____

Assess Comprehension and Vocabulary

A. Read the following passage. Think about the main idea and details.

World War I lasted from 1914 to 1918. Millions of lives were lost. However, from 1918 to 1919, a disease killed more than twice as many people. This disease was influenza. Between 20 and 40 million people did not survive the influenza pandemic. A pandemic is an outbreak of an illness throughout the world. The disease was everywhere. Children jumped rope to a popular rhyme:

> *I had a little bird,*
> *Its name was Enza.*
> *I opened the window,*
> *And in-flu-enza.*

From your experience, you might think the flu is as harmless as the common cold. Yet, this flu was strong. Most people could not tolerate the effects. People died within hours of getting sick. They would struggle to breathe. Their noses and mouths became blocked by gruesome and bloody phlegm, and they would suffocate. Many soldiers, still on the battlefield as the war was winding down, got the flu. Because many doctors were needed to care for the wounded and sick soldiers, civilians at home in the United States had fewer doctors to care for them. Instead of a doctor, nurses might prescribe medicine for patients. American Red Cross volunteers provided treatment to an increasing number of patients.

B. Circle the letter of each correct answer.

1. What is the BEST definition of the word *survive*?
   A. become ill during
   B. stay alive through
   C. cause danger in
   D. take medicine for

2. Which word is a synonym for *tolerate*?
   A. weaken
   B. find
   C. annoy
   D. bear

3. Which word is an antonym for *gruesome*?
   A. disgusting
   B. putrid
   C. pleasant
   D. horrible

4. Which word does NOT go with *prescribe*?
   A. annoy
   B. medicine
   C. treatment
   D. write

Name _____ **Date** _____

5. Which thing is NOT a *treatment*?

   A. remedy

   B. germs

   C. medicine

   D. cure

6. What would be a good title for the passage?

   A. On the Battlefronts of World War I

   B. The Deadliest Flu

   C. Survivors of the Year 1918

   D. Volunteers of the American Red Cross

7. What is the topic of this passage?

   A. prescriptions for the flu

   B. the bird flu

   C. the flu pandemic of 1918

   D. World War I

8. Which statement from the passage is FALSE?

   A. Nurses weren't allowed to give prescriptions.

   B. The flu caused some people to suffocate.

   C. More people died from the flu in 1918 than in World War I.

   D. Many soldiers got the flu.

9. Which detail does NOT show the seriousness of influenza?

   A. People died within hours of getting the flu.

   B. The flu caused twice as many deaths as World War I.

   C. People with the flu suffocated.

   D. Children jumped rope to a popular rhyme about the flu.

10. Use the main idea and important details to write a brief passage summary with at least three sentences.

   _____

   _____

   _____

   _____

   _____

   _____

   _____

   _____

   _____

   _____

   _____

   _____

   _____

   _____

   _____

Name _____   Date _____

C. Read the following passage. Think about the main idea and details.

> Have you ever wanted to become better at studying or exercising? Many people develop good habits and change habits that are bad for them. Why are they successful? They choose a plan and stick with it. Some people focus on one change for 30 days and pay attention to triggers. For example, if you wanted to stop eating sweets, you would snap your fingers every time you want to buy a candy bar. The trigger is the urge to eat sweets, and you snap to call special attention to it and stop it. After a while, your mind and body stop sending the urge, and you've changed a bad habit. Yet, you need to replace the good feelings that the old habit gave you. If you give up watching television, you should find a new way to relax or get information.

D. Circle the letter of each correct answer.

11. What is the topic of this passage?

    A. health habits

    B. changing habits

    C. study habits

    D. bad habits

12. The main idea of the passage . . .

    A. is stated directly.

    B. is not stated directly.

    C. has no details to support it.

    D. is state explicitly.

13. What is the main idea of the passage?

    A. You can change a habit if you try.

    B. People can develop or change habits by using a plan.

    C. The 30-day plan is the only way to change a habit.

    D. If you use a trigger to change a habit, you will succeed.

14. How does the following sentence support the main idea?

    Some people focus on one change for 30 days and pay attention to triggers.

    A. It tells what people should not do to change a habit.

    B. It is an example of a bad habit.

    C. It is an example of a plan for changing a habit.

    D. It tells the benefit of a good habit.

15. What does the passage imply, or not state directly?

    A. Developing a new habit should make you feel good.

    B. You have to be an expert to change or develop a habit.

    C. Changing a habit takes a short time.

    D. Most people watch television too much.

Name _____   Date _____

Reteach

A. You can determine the main idea of a passage when it is stated indirectly. Follow these steps.

1. Read the passage.
2. Underline important words and phrases as you read.
3. Answer the questions.

Have you ever wanted to go back in time? A visit to Colonial Williamsburg is just the ticket. Williamsburg is in the state of Virginia. Virginia used to be one of the 13 British Colonies. In Williamsburg, many original historic homes and buildings still stand. Some buildings look just as they did many years ago. You can visit the capitol building, the Governor's Palace, Bruton Parish Church, and the Raleigh Tavern. The people who work in historical Williamsburg dress, work, and talk as if it is the 18th century. You might see a tailor sitting in his shop window as he stitches a gentleman's colonial-era jacket. You also may talk with a gardener who grows the same flowers and herbs that colonists grew. Sometimes, there are reenactments of historic events. You might even catch a glimpse of soldiers recreating a Revolutionary War battle. Stepping inside history might be the most exciting way to learn about it.

---

1. Reread the first four sentences. What are they about?

   _____
   _____

2. The rest of the sentences appeal to your sense of sight. Describe two pictures you see in your mind.

   _____
   _____
   _____
   _____
   _____

3. Write four important words or phrases from the passage.

   _____
   _____
   _____

4. Decide what the topic of the passage is. State the topic in one word or a few words.

   _____

5. Find three important details. Make sure the details connect to the topic. Write them in short sentences.

   _____
   _____
   _____
   _____
   _____
   _____
   _____

Name _____   Date _____

6. The main idea is not directly stated in the passage. It is implicit. When you state the implicit main idea, use a complete sentence. Use the following sentence starter to state the passage main idea.

   You can visit Colonial Williamsburg to _____

   _____.

B. Use the important details and the main idea to write a brief passage summary. Your summary should be at least three sentences.

   _____

   _____

   _____

   _____

   _____

   _____

   _____

   _____

Name _____   Date _____

Are Dreadlocks for You?

Several months ago, I made the decision to wear my hair in dreadlocks.

I started my dreadlocks then, and I've been growing and twisting them ever since. Dreadlocks are a natural hairstyle in which hair is twisted into matted or ropelike locks. Some dreadlocks are thin and neat; others are thick and look messy. Dreadlocks create a distinctive look, and they require special care.

A Brief History of Dreadlocks

Dreadlocks, also called *dreads* or *locks* (often spelled *locs*), are not a recent fashion trend. In fact, they have been around for centuries. Cultures from Egypt to India to Greece to Jamaica have adopted dreadlocks at different points in time. Dreadlocks often have been the hairstyle of choice for religious worshippers who are devoted to living lives without excess or comfort.

Why Choose Dreadlocks?

People choose to wear dreadlocks for a number of different reasons. In modern times, dreadlocks often are worn as part of Rastafarian religious practice. Rastafarianism is a religion and political movement that originated in Jamaica. Among other practices, Rastafarianism is based on a philosophy of simplicity. Additionally, dreadlocks have become a political statement against mainstream culture. For some people, dreadlocks are simply a hairstyle choice based on popular trends. Each person who chooses dreadlocks will have his or her own reasons. I decided that I wanted locks because I wanted to wear a symbol of my African heritage.

Proper Care of Dreadlocks

Dreadlocks can be mysterious to people who have never worn them, so I will share with you what I've learned about taking care of locks. Each person's locks have his or her own "personality" based on hair texture and care, but this is what worked for me.

Name _____ Date _____

- Dreadlocks form from hair naturally knotting. The oils in your hair will help keep the different locks separate. You can start your locks either on your own or at a salon. I started my own dreads. First, I separated my hair into sections. Next, I combed each section to be as frizzy as possible. Then, I twisted the sections into ropes. Finally, I used a special wax to seal and separate my locks.

- Some people say it's important not to wash your hair for the first four to six weeks while your locks are forming. I know if you have gym class or participate in sports, it may not be practical to keep your hair dry for four to six weeks. You don't have to go without washing your hair. Instead, you can use a special shampoo that doesn't contain conditioners and detanglers.

- Be sure to dry your locks thoroughly when they get wet. Mold can actually grow inside locks if they remain damp. Mold starts to smell really bad.

- Keep your scalp healthy. If you experience itchiness, take care of it immediately. I use hair oils on my scalp to keep it from getting too dry.

- Remember that locks are generally a permanent style that can't be combed out. To remove locks, you will need to cut them off.

Use the information you marked in the passage to summarize the article. Your summary should be at least three sentences.

_____

_____

_____

_____

_____

_____

_____

_____

_____

_____

Name _____   Date _____

Exploring Careers: Phlebotomists

A. Answer the following questions about a career as a phlebotomist.

1. What are two reasons a phlebotomist draws blood?

    _____

2. What are three different places where a phlebotomist can work?

    _____

3. What are skills and abilities a phlebotomist needs?

    _____

    _____

4. What are the educational requirements for becoming a phlebotomist?

    _____

    _____

    _____

5. Is the need for phlebotomists high? Explain.

    _____

    _____

    _____

    _____

B. Use the Internet to research other possible career choices in this field and complete the chart.

Career	
Responsibilities	
Education Required	
Average Salary	
Is this a career you might pursue?	
Why or why not?	
Career	
Responsibilities	
Education Required	
Average Salary	
Is this a career you might pursue?	
Why or why not?	

Name _____   Date _____

Vocabulary

"Curious Customs"

A. Rate your knowledge of each boldfaced word.

3   I know what this word means, and I can use it in a sentence.
2   I have an idea of this word's meaning, but I need to know more.
1   I don't know what this word means.

☐   **contemporary** (adj) *at the present time*
    Some colonial-era customs are still in practice in *contemporary* times.

☐   **qualified** (adj) *fit for a given purpose*
    When a young man learned a trade, he was *qualified* to work on his own.

☐   **instruct** (v) *teach*
    A shoemaker could *instruct* someone on how to make and repair shoes.

☐   **transaction** (n) *an exchange of goods, services, or money*
    Working for a tradesman in exchange for learning a good trade was a common *transaction*.

☐   **various** (adj) *of differing kinds; representing a variety*
    Just like today, teenagers in colonial times needed *various* skills.

☐   **society** (n) *people living together as a group with the same way of life*
    Do you think colonial *society* was very different from the way we live now?

B. Read each statement. Circle true or false.

1. If you have **various** talents, you are good at just one thing.   true   false

2. If you **instruct** someone, you tell him or her how to do something.   true   false

3. If you are a good cook, you might be **qualified** to work as a chef.   true   false

4. The printing press is a **contemporary** invention.   true   false

5. In today's **society**, men and women cannot go to large sports events together.   true   false

6. Buying a movie ticket is a common **transaction** that many people do often. true   false

Name _____   Date _____

Word Building

A. Some suffixes can change the part of speech. The suffix *-ion*, which means "act of, state of, or result of," can change verbs to nouns. Read the following words and their meanings.

Verbs	
transact	*do business*
instruct	*teach*
irritate	*annoy or bother*
compensate	*pay for work*
motivate	*move to action*

+ *-ion*

Nouns	
transaction	*an exchange of goods, services, or money; a business deal*
instruction	*act or process of teaching*
irritation	*the state of being bothered; something that bothers*
compensation	*money received for work*
motivation	*something that inspires action*

B. Choose a verb or noun from Part A to complete each sentence.

1. Our swim teacher gave us a book of safety _____.

2. My cat likes to _____ me by pawing at me early in the morning.

3. Ms. Grassley said she would _____ us well for the work we did.

4. The coach's can-do attitude was great _____ for the team.

5. The blue jay is a pretty bird, but its loud squawk is an _____.

6. When I buy something at the store, the _____ is complete when the cashier hands me the receipt.

7. To _____ us, our coach gives pep talks at halftime.

8. We received _____ for mowing the neighbor's yard.

9. I wish a famous basketball player could _____ me in making a three-point basket.

10. My mother went inside the bank to _____ with the bank teller.

Name _____   Date _____

Inference

Read the bold statements from "Curious Customs." Then, make an inference about each statement.

Treatment of women under the law reflected their status.

What I Read		What I Already Know		Inference
I read this about the treatment women received:	**+**	I know that women in today's society . . .	**=**	So, I think the status of women in the 18th century was . . .

You can get a good sense of manners in the 18th century from two of Washington's guidelines.

What I Read		What I Already Know		Inference
I read this about Washington's guidelines:	**+**	I know that people in today's society . . .	**=**	So, my sense of manners in the 18th century is . . .

Name _____   Date _____

Write in Response to Reading

Imagine a passage about today's customs—but written 100 years from now. Which of your common activities will someone in the future think are "curious customs"? Which customs will last into the 22nd century? Which customs will be totally new?

Curious Customs of the 21st Century

_____
_____
_____
_____
_____
_____

Lasting Customs

_____
_____
_____
_____
_____
_____
_____
_____
_____

Totally New Customs

_____
_____
_____
_____
_____
_____
_____
_____

Name _____ Date _____

Vocabulary

"Teen Life—Blast to the Past"

A. Write one or more numbers next to each boldfaced word to show when you have seen, heard, or used this word.

5   I use it in everyday conversation.
4   I heard it on TV or on the radio.
3   I heard or used it in school.
2   I read it in a book, magazine, or online.
1   I have not read, heard, or used this word.

activities (n) *things you do*
Playing sports and watching TV are common *activities*.

fundamental (adj) *basic or main; serving as the basis*
Reading and math are *fundamental* parts of any education.

crucial (adj) *important*
An education is *crucial* if you want to be successful.

employment (n) *a person's work; job*
Many people found *employment* in mills and factories.

social (adj) *having to do with people coming together in a friendly group*
Events where people gather are often *social* events.

B. Read each question, then write the answer on the line.

1. If you are involved in several **activities**, are you busy or bored? _____

2. Are the rules of a game **fundamental** or unnecessary? _____

3. Would a **crucial** decision be important or unimportant? _____

4. Do you play or work in your place of **employment**? _____

5. If you are at a **social** gathering, are you alone or with other people? _____

C. Choose two words from Part A. Use each word in a sentence.

1. _____

_____

2. _____

_____

Name _____ Date _____

Word Building

A. Many words have Greek or Latin roots. The word *social* means "having to do with people coming together in a friendly group." The Latin root *socialis* means "of companionship or friendship." Read the following words that use the root *socialis* and notice what they have in common with the idea of companionship.

Words	Definitions
society	*people living together as a group with the same way of life*
socialize	*take part in social activities*
sociology	*the study of human social behavior*
socialism	*an economic system based on public ownership and control of land, factories, food, and goods*

B. Complete each sentence with one of the words in Part A.

1. In a society that practices _____, the people share ownership of resources.

2. We live in a _____ that uses complicated technology.

3. My sister is studying group behavior in her _____ class.

4. On holidays, most people like to _____ with friends and family members.

C. *Employment* means "a person's work or job." The base word is *employ*, which means "make use of." By adding suffixes and prefixes to *employ,* you can create other words. Use your affixionary to identify prefixes and suffixes and complete the following chart. The first one is done for you.

Word	Prefix	Suffix	Definition
employee		**-ee**	*one employed by another*
employer			
		-able	able to be employed
unemployable			
	un-	-ed	without a job
unemployment			

Name _____   Date _____

Text Features

Use text features in "Teen Life—Blast to the Past" to locate the text described in the Locate column of the chart. In the second column, write the text features that helped you locate the information. In the last column, use the passage text to retell the information you located.

Locate	What text features helped?	Retell Important Information
Information about young women and men going to work in mills and factories		
Information about education		
Text that tells about how and why jobs for teens changed		
Text that tells about social activities		
Text that compares the past with today		Discuss the comparisons and contrasts mentioned in the text with a partner.

Name _____   Date _____

Write in Response to Reading

A. Imagine the apprenticeships in "Teen Life—Blast to the Past" still exist. Make a decision about your future. Read your options in the chart. Then, make the crucial decisions to plan your future by listing the pros (good things about the job) and the cons (bad or negative things).

Jobs	Pros	Cons
Computer technician who repairs people's computers		
Dressmaker working for a designer		
A plumber's helper working for a plumber		

B. Choose an apprenticeship that you would like to have from Part A. Describe what you think you will learn and what your experience will be like.

_____

_____

_____

_____

_____

_____

_____

_____

_____

_____

_____

_____

_____

_____

Name _____   Date _____

Review Vocabulary

A. Complete each sentence with a word from the box.

society	contemporary	compensation	employment
qualified	agricultural	various	activities

> Someone from the 18th century would probably think that many of our _____
>
> customs are odd. _____ has changed a lot in 300 years. For one thing, more
>
> people live and work in cities today, and fewer people live in _____ areas.
>
> Anyone from the past would marvel at the amount of _____ most workers
>
> earn today. They also might be stunned by the _____ kinds of
>
> _____ workers can choose today. Of course, people need a high level of
>
> education and training to become _____ to work at some of those jobs.

B. Choose one business or product and write an advertisement for it below. Use at least five bold words from the box in your advertisement.

Flying Feet Dance School   **Kline Construction Company**   **Clean and Bright Shampoo**

instruct	**apprenticed**	**fundamental**	**crucial**
transaction	**activities**	**repetitive**	**social**

Name _____ Date _____

Extend Vocabulary

A. When you see words in word families, the definition of one word can help you understand the definition of other words. Prefix and suffix meanings are other clues you can use. Use a dictionary to complete the following chart. Add examples.

Word Families	Definitions	Examples
qualify		
qualified	*fit for a given purpose*	
qualification		several years of experience in repairing motorcycles
instruct	*teach*	
instruction		
instructor		
employ		
employment	*a person's work; a job*	
employer		
apprentice		
apprenticed	*trained by a professional*	
apprenticeship		situation of learning as you work in a carpenter business

B. Complete each sentence with one of the words from Part A.

1. A photographer's _____ will learn how to use and maintain cameras.

2. Our _____ in science class taught the safety rules before starting the experiment.

3. A high school diploma is a basic _____ for almost any job.

4. My _____ said it would be okay for me to miss work next Saturday.

5. Will knowing how to read music _____ me to be in the band?

Name _____   Date _____

Assess Comprehension and Vocabulary

A. Read the passage. Use what you already know and what you read in the passage to make inferences.

> Olivia Miller was happy to have employment in the milliner's shop. She loved feeling the thick textures of brocade and the cool smoothness of fine silks between her fingers. Whenever new fabrics arrived, like today, her imagination took over. She could see Mrs. Henry in a gown made of the yellow chintz or Mr. Hadley in a coat from the dark blue wool. She went so far as to choose the various items that each would need to complete the outfit. Mr. Hadley would certainly need a new hat, and Mrs. Hadley should have a contemporary pin. The jewelry would look nice pinned to the gown at its neckline. Olivia knew just which pin she would choose from the jewelry counter.
>
> Miss Landon, the owner of the shop, was quick to end Olivia's dreaming. "Snap! Snap!" she would say. "There's no time for daydreaming. Mrs. Caine will be in at 9 o'clock for her fitting. Hurry now and finish stitching the hem of her dress. Remember that she likes her skirt just a little shorter than most customers. She says that longer skirts get dirtier quicker. She won't tolerate any mistakes."
>
> Olivia went straight to her task, but she continued daydreaming. As she worked with her needle and thread, she dreamed of the day when she would be qualified to have her own name on a sign hanging over a milliner's shop.

B. Circle the letter of each correct answer.

1. Which word does NOT go with *qualified*?
   A. experienced
   B. trained
   C. skilled
   D. unskilled

2. Which definition BEST fits the word *contemporary*?
   A. exchange of goods for money
   B. ways of doing things or traditions
   C. at the present time
   D. jewelry that is pinned on clothing

3. Which of these things has *various* parts?
   A. wristwatch
   B. plate
   C. comb
   D. paper clip

4. Which word is a synonym for *tolerate*?
   A. trust
   B. bear
   C. reject
   D. complain

Name _____   Date _____

5. Which word is a synonym for *employment*?
    A. compensation
    B. school
    C. job
    D. salary

6. Which profession in today's world would Olivia MOST LIKELY pursue?
    A. seamstress
    B. textile artist
    C. fashion designer
    D. model

7. What are brocade and silk?
    A. colors
    B. fabrics
    C. dresses
    D. accessories

8. What other kinds of cloth are mentioned in the passage?
    A. cotton and linen
    B. nylon and wool
    C. chintz and wool
    D. gown and skirt

9. What can you infer about Olivia's position or title at the milliner's shop?
    A. She is Miss Landon's apprentice.
    B. She is the owner of the shop.
    C. She is a customer in the shop.
    D. She delivers fabric to the shop.

10. Which text feature or features would NOT be helpful in this passage?
    A. illustration
    B. title
    C. graph
    D. paragraph headings

11. When you infer, you use what you read and what you already know to figure out what the passage does not state directly. Read the following sentence. What can you infer?
    She loved feeling the thick textures of brocade and the cool smoothness of fine silks between her fingers.
    A. Silk comes only in cool colors like blues and greens.
    B. The shop has fabrics in many styles, textures, and weights.
    C. Olivia does not pay much attention to the fabrics in the shop.
    D. Brocade and silk are the best fabrics for making dresses.

Name _____   Date _____

12. Read the following sentences. What can you infer about the town where Mrs. Caine lives?

    Remember that she (Mrs. Caine) likes her skirt just a little shorter than most customers. She says that longer skirts get dirtier quicker.

    A. The town is modern and clean.

    B. The weather there is hot.

    C. The town has dirty, unpaved streets.

    D. Women wear heavy clothing to protect themselves from the weather.

13. Read the following sentence. What is Olivia's plan for the future?

    She dreamed of the day when she would be qualified to have her own name on a sign hanging over a milliner's shop.

    A. She will own her own shop one day.

    B. She will learn how to sew on a machine.

    C. She will be Miss Landon's boss one day.

    D. She will someday wear silk dresses.

14. Read the following statements. Which statement BEST describes Miss Landon?

    A. Miss Landon is easygoing.

    B. Miss Landon has a good sense of humor.

    C. Miss Landon wants to keep her customers happy.

    D. Miss Landon is patient.

15. Read the following statements. Which statement BEST describes Olivia?

    A. She is ambitious and eager to learn.

    B. She is forgetful and lazy.

    C. She does not have plans for her future.

    D. She wants to work in jewelry store.

Name _____ Date _____

Reteach

A. Read the passage and poster. Think about what you read as you answer the questions.

In the 1930s, the United States was in an economic depression. Banks and other businesses closed. Thousands of people lost their jobs. Many of them lost their homes. People were looking for a better life with more opportunity and more promise. California seemed to offer both. To people with nothing left to lose, California offered a new life.

1. What is a good title for this passage?

   _____

2. What is an economic depression?

   _____

   _____

3. Why did California seem to offer both opportunity and promise?

   _____

4. Why were people looking for a better life?

   _____

5. Why did people lose their homes?

   _____

6. What was the weather like in California? How do you know?

   _____

   _____

7. What does the poster call California?

   _____

Name _____ Date _____

B. You read a lot of information in the passage and poster. Add what you already know to make inferences.

I read and learned . . .	I already know . . .	So I infer that . . .
California had a lot of land.	People can use land to farm.	Many people would want to get the land in California.
In the 1930s, the United States was in an economic depression.	During an economic depression,	Many people at that time wanted
Millions of immigrants were in California.	As some immigrants find jobs, they might tell their families and	In the 1930s,
The weather in California was temperate, and the seasons were pleasant.	When the weather is nice, people expect	So,
California was called the "Cornucopia of the World."	A cornucopia looks like	So,

C. Write a brief summary of the main idea of the text and the poster. Begin with the main idea. Then, give two details that support the statement. Last, write your own inference about the information.

_____

_____

_____

_____

_____

_____

_____

Name _____ Date _____

Real World—E-Mail Forward

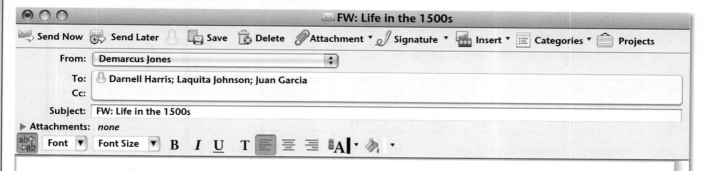

FW: Life in the 1500s

Send Now   Send Later   Save   Delete   Attachment ▾   Signature ▾   Insert ▾   Categories ▾   Projects

From: Demarcus Jones

To: Darnell Harris; Laquita Johnson; Juan Garcia
Cc:

Subject: FW: Life in the 1500s

▶ Attachments: *none*

Font ▾   Font Size ▾   B   I   U   T   ≡ ≡ ≡   A ▾   ⬧ ▾

Hey, I got this from my cousin in Memphis. Check it out. I wish they'd put this kind of stuff in our history book.

Peace, D

LIFE IN THE 1500s

Most people got married in June because they took their yearly bath in May, so they still smelled pretty good by June. However, they were starting to smell, so brides carried a bouquet of flowers to hide the body odor. So, brides have the custom today of carrying a bouquet when getting married.

Baths consisted of a big tub filled with hot water. The man of the house had the privilege of the clean water, then all the other adult men, then the women, and finally the children. Last of all, the babies were bathed. By then, the water was so dirty you could actually lose someone in it. Hence the saying, "Don't throw out the baby with the bathwater."

Houses had thatched roofs, which were thick straw piled high with no wood underneath. It was the only place for animals to get warm, so the cats and dogs lived on the roof. When it rained, it became slippery, and sometimes the animals would slip and fall off the roof. That's why we say, "It's raining cats and dogs."

Other small animals, including mice and bugs, also lived on the roof. With these thatched roofs, nothing stopped things from falling into the house. This posed a real problem in the bedroom where bugs and other droppings could mess up your nice clean bed. So, a bed with big posts and a sheet hung over the top afforded some protection. That's how canopy beds came into existence.

The floor was dirt. Only the wealthy had something other than dirt. Hence, the saying, "He's dirt poor." The wealthy had slate floors that would get slippery in the winter when wet, so they spread thresh, or straw, on the floor to help them keep their footing. As the winter wore on, they added more thresh until it would all start blowing outside when you opened the door. So, they placed a piece of wood in the entranceway. That entranceway is now called a threshold.

(Getting quite an education, aren't you?)

In those days, they cooked with a big kettle that always hung over the fire. Every day they lit the fire and added food to the pot. They ate mostly vegetables and did not get much meat. They would eat the stew for dinner, leaving leftovers in the pot to get cold overnight and then start over the next

Name _____ Date _____

○ ○ ○   ✉ FW: Life in the 1500s

Send Now   Send Later   ⎙ Save   🗑 Delete   ⊘ Attachment ▾   ✎ Signature ▾   🏢 Insert ▾   ☰ Categories ▾   🗐 Projects

From: Demarcus Jones   ⬍

To: 👤 Darnell Harris; Laquita Johnson; Juan Garcia

Cc:

Subject: FW: Life in the 1500s

▸ Attachments: *none*

abc✓   Font ▾   Font Size ▾   **B**   *I*   U   T   ☰ ≡ ≡   ▤A▾   🖌▾

day. Sometimes the stew contained food that had been there for quite a while. That's how the rhyme, "Peas porridge hot, peas porridge cold, peas porridge in the pot nine days old," originated.

Sometimes they could obtain pork, which made them feel quite special. When visitors came over, they hung up their bacon to show off. It was a sign of wealth that a man could "bring home the bacon." They would cut off a little to share with guests and would all sit around and "chew the fat."

Those with money had plates made of pewter. Food with high acid content caused some of the lead to leach into the food, causing fatal lead poisoning. This happened most often with tomatoes because they are very acidic. So, for the next 400 years or so, tomatoes were considered poisonous.

Bread was divided according to status. Workers got the burnt bottom of the loaf, the family got the middle, and guests or high society folk got the top, or the upper crust. That is why some refer to high society people as "the upper crust."

Lead cups were used to drink ale or whiskey. The combination of lead and alcohol would sometimes knock a person out for a couple of days. Someone walking along the road would take them for dead and prepare them for burial. They were laid out on the kitchen table for a couple of days, and the family would gather around and eat and drink and wait and see if they would wake up. That is where we get the custom of holding a wake.

England was small, and the local folks started running out of places to bury people. So they would dig up coffins, take the bones to a bone-house, and reuse the grave. When reopening these coffins, one out of 25 coffins was found to have scratch marks on the inside. They realized they had been burying people alive. So they would tie a string on the wrist of the corpse, lead it through the coffin and up through the ground, and tie it to a bell. Someone would have to sit out in the graveyard all night (the graveyard shift) to listen for the bell. Thus, someone could be "saved by the bell" or be considered "a dead ringer."

That's the truth. Whoever said history is boring? Educate someone. Share these facts with a friend.

Before you share these facts, you need to know that only one is actually true. Which one do you think is correct?

_____

_____

_____

Name _____   Date _____

Exploring Careers: Museum Curator

A. Answer the following questions about a career as a museum curator.

1. What are the three main jobs of a museum curator?

   _____

2. Name three places where you could see the work of a museum curator.

   _____

3. Why does a museum curator need to know about art and design?

   _____

   _____

4. What education do most museum curators have?

   _____

   _____

5. What is the salary for a museum curator?

   _____

   _____

B. Use the Internet to research other possible career choices in this field and complete the chart.

Career	
Responsibilities	
Education Required	
Average Salary	
Is this a career you might pursue?	
Why or why not?	
Career	
Responsibilities	
Education Required	
Average Salary	
Is this a career you might pursue?	
Why or why not?	

Name _____   Date _____

A. Organize Your Ideas

The Future of Our Past

-
-
-

How does fiction shape the future?

-
-
-

What does the future hold for us?

-
-
-

What possibilities of the future are scary?

-
-
-

What else would you like to know about future possibilities?

_____

_____

B. The Big Picture

Write the big idea of each passage in the outside ovals. Connect the passages in the center oval by writing the big picture.

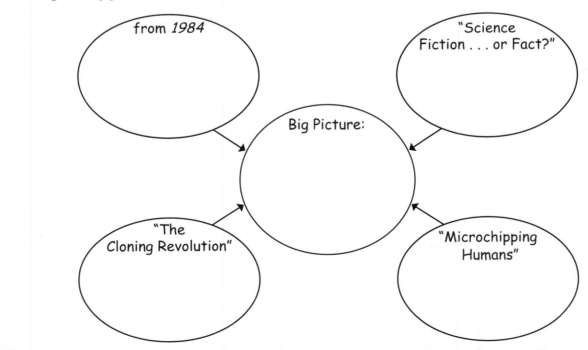

from *1984*

"Science Fiction . . . or Fact?"

Big Picture:

"The Cloning Revolution"

"Microchipping Humans"

C. Expedition Dictionary

You will read the following vocabulary words throughout the Expedition. As you learn the words, use them as often as possible in your oral and written language.

from *1984*

nuzzled	(v) *put close to something*
vile	(adj) *low in worth; unpleasant*
depicted	(v) *showed something in a picture or by using words*
seldom	(adv) *rarely; not often*
contrived	(v) *formed or created in a specific way*
frail	(adj) *weak*

"Science Fiction . . . or Fact?"

predict	(v) *declare that something is going to happen in the future*
coincidence	(n) *when things happen by accident and are not connected to each other*
develop	(v) *work out the possibilities of something*
reaction	(n) *a response to something*
elaborate	(adj) *very detailed*
devices	(n) *pieces of equipment that serve a special purpose*

"The Cloning Revolution"

typically	(adv) *how things usually are; generally*
deliberate	(adj) *planned or intended*
replicate	(v) *make a copy of; duplicate*
intense	(adj) *involving or showing extreme effort*
differentiate	(v) *show a difference between two things*
generated	(v) *produced; created*

"Microchipping Humans"

convenience	(n) *something that is useful and easy to use*
debate	(v) *discuss something*
conform	(v) *act in an expected way*
standards	(n) *rules or models used to judge how good something is*
cautious	(adj) *tries to avoid mistakes or danger*
regulates	(v) *controls or manages*

Dictionary Challenge

Create a diary entry of a day in your life in 2035 using as many vocabulary words as possible.

Name _____ Date _____

Vocabulary

from *1984*

A. Write one or more numbers next to each boldfaced word to show when you have seen, heard, or used this word.

5 I use it in everyday conversation.
4 I heard it on TV or on the radio.
3 I heard or used it in school.
2 I read it in a book, magazine, or online.
1 I have not read, heard, or used this word.

☐ **nuzzled** (v) *put close to something*
Winston kept his face *nuzzled* into his chest to avoid being noticed.

☐ **vile** (adj) *low in worth; unpleasant*
The *vile* city looked horrible from the window.

☐ **depicted** (v) *showed something in a picture or by using words*
The painting *depicted* a man with a mustache.

☐ **seldom** (adv) *rarely; not often*
Because he was being watched, Winston *seldom* did anything wrong.

☐ **contrived** (v) *formed or created in a specific way*
The rules were *contrived* to keep people from meeting to discuss the government.

☐ **frail** (adj) *weak*
He looked *frail* because he had not eaten much lately.

B. Read each statement. Circle true or false.

1. When a pet has **nuzzled** into your hand, it has bitten you.   true   false

2. Warm, sunny weather would be considered **vile**.   true   false

3. A person's face may be **depicted** in a painting.   true   false

4. If you are healthy and exercise regularly, you will become **frail**.   true   false

5. If you **seldom** practice guitar, you will become an expert.   true   false

6. If someone **contrived** a secret code, that person might be able to trick other people.   true   false

Name _____   Date _____

Visualize and Predict

Examine the following photo. Imagine yourself in the place of one of the characters. Visualize the scene from that character's perspective. Answer the questions.

Choose either the boy or the father. Visualize the events from that perspective.

1. What would you see? _____
   _____
   _____
   _____

2. What would you smell? _____
   _____
   _____

3. What would you hear? _____
   _____
   _____
   _____

4. What emotions would you feel?
   _____
   _____

5. What do you visualize about the rest of the house and outdoors?

   _____
   _____
   _____
   _____

6. Predict what happens next.

   _____
   _____
   _____
   _____

Name _____   Date _____

Word Building

A. For each vocabulary word, write either *S* for a synonym or *A* for an antonym. Use a dictionary if necessary.

frail	_____ weak	_____ strong	_____ delicate
vile	_____ disgusting	_____ horrible	_____ pleasant
seldom	_____ rarely	_____ frequently	_____ not often
contrived	_____ made	_____ built	_____ destroyed
depicted	_____ portrayed	_____ hid	_____ represented

B. Think about the meanings of the boldfaced words in Part A and how you have heard each word used. Complete each sentence with a word from the list.

1. In *1984*, the government _____ telescreens that heard everything you said.

2. If you knew you were being watched all the time, you would _____ disobey the law.

3. Lack of food made Winston appear _____.

4. The leader's harsh features were clearly _____ in the poster.

5. Unlike the sunny south, the northern winters are cold and _____.

C. Define *nuzzled* and use it in a sentence.

_____

_____

D. Complete the sentences about the future. Use a vocabulary word in each sentence.

1. In the future, _____

_____.

2. In the future, _____

_____.

Name _____   Date _____

Visualize and Predict

A. Read the text quote, and underline the words that describe the scene. Then, draw the picture you created in your mind.

Text Quote	Visualize
"At one end of [the hallway] a colored poster . . . depicted simply an enormous face . . . of a man of about forty-five, with a heavy black mustache and ruggedly handsome features . . . BIG BROTHER IS WATCHING YOU, the caption beneath it ran."	
"Were there always these vistas of rotting nineteenth-century houses, their sides shored up with balks of timber, their windows patched with cardboard and their roofs with corrugated iron, their crazy garden walls sagging in all directions?"	
"The Ministry of Truth . . . was an enormous pyramidal structure of glittering white concrete, soaring up, terrace after terrace, three hundred meters into the air . . . on its white face in elegant lettering, the three slogans of the Party: WAR IS PEACE FREEDOM IS SLAVERY IGNORANCE IS STRENGTH."	

B. Complete each sentence with your own idea.

1. After reading the text and visualizing the scenes, I can predict that Winston will _____
   _____.

2. If I were a member of the society Winston lives in, I would _____
   _____.

Name _____   **Date** _____

Write in Response to Reading

Imagine you have been offered a great new job. It pays well and is close to home, and you like what you will do. This business believes in monitoring its employees. There are video cameras in all the offices, hallways, stairwells, break rooms, and elevators. Each computer is outfitted with a webcam so you can be monitored at your desk. Would you want to work for this company? Would you mind being monitored? Write a letter to your new employer explaining whether you will accept the job and how you feel about being monitored.

Dear _____,

_____

_____

_____

_____

_____

_____

_____

_____

_____

_____

_____

_____

_____

_____

_____

_____

_____

_____

_____

_____

_____

_____

_____

Sincerely,

_____

Name _____ Date _____

Vocabulary

"Science Fiction . . . or Fact?"

A. Rate your knowledge of each boldfaced word.

3 I know what this word means, and I can use it in a sentence.
2 I have an idea of this word's meaning, but I need to know more.
1 I don't know what this word means.

☐   **predict**   (v) *declare that something is going to happen in the future*
They *predict* that people in the future will drive air cars.

☐   **coincidence**   (n) *when things happen by accident and are not connected to each other*
Were flip phones designed to look like the devices on *Star Trek*, or is it a *coincidence*?

☐   **develop**   (v) *work out the possibilities of something*
Science fiction writers *develop* ideas for transportation and communication in the future.

☐   **reaction**   (n) *a response to something*
Her *reaction* to science fiction ideas is disbelief.

☐   **elaborate**   (adj) *very detailed*
Most science fiction creatures have *elaborate* features and costumes.

☐   **devices**   (n) *pieces of equipment that serve a special purpose*
Many electronic *devices* are designed to make life easier.

B. Read each question, then write the answer on the line.

1. Could you **predict** an event that happened in the past or one that will happen in the future?

   _____

2. Would it be a **coincidence** if you planned to meet a friend at the library or if you both wanted to check out the same book? _____

3. If you wanted to **develop** a new type of contact lens, would you test different ways of making them or buy them as a present? _____

4. Would your **reaction** to winning a million-dollar prize be frustration or excitement?

   _____

5. If you created an **elaborate** drawing of a weather control machine, would it have many details or few? _____

6. Are examples of **devices** cell phones or sales associates? _____

Name _____ Date _____

Word Building

A. *Develop* means "work out the possibilities of something."

> People invent and *develop* ideas that we once thought were impossible.

The word *develop* also can mean "adopt or acquire."

> You can *develop* healthy habits by getting enough sleep, eating nutritional meals, and exercising regularly.

Another meaning for *develop* is "arise and increase."

> Disagreements between workers and unions often *develop* into strikes.

B. Choose *1*, *2*, or *3* to identify the meaning of the boldfaced word in each sentence.
develop
1. work out the possibilities of something
2. adopt or acquire
3. arise and increase

_____ 1. The tropical storm will **develop** into a hurricane by nightfall.

_____ 2. The company has plans to **develop** a technology that has just been discovered.

_____ 3. You can **develop** a hearing loss if you listen to music that is too loud.

_____ 4. Many families **develop** ideas to save money and stick to a budget.

_____ 5. Illnesses **develop** as a result of improper medical treatment.

C. When people use devices, inventions, and machines, they often use words that have the base word *active*. Answer the questions using your knowledge of affixes.

1. What device can you **activate**? _____

2. How can you **deactivate** something? _____

3. What group of people might get ready for **activation**? _____

_____

4. What **reaction** would you have if someone pointed a TASER at you? _____

Name _____   Date _____

Visualize and Predict

Reread the text, noting descriptions of each idea. Write a few words that help you visualize the item in the past. Next, write a few words to describe the object as it is used today. Finally, predict how the item will develop in the future. Draw a picture to support your prediction.

	Then	Now	Future Prediction	Drawing
Forms of Payment	1888: metal coins; credit written on paper	Current Year:		
Television	1953:	Current Year:		
Weapons	1911:	Current Year:		
Space Travel	1865: Space travel was inexistent.	Current Year:		

Name _____   Date _____

Write in Response to Reading

If you could invent a futuristic product, what would it be? Name your product or new technology and sketch it below. After you produce it, you need to persuade the public to buy your product. Write five main scenes of a 30-minute infomercial program to air on television. Include information about what the product or technology does and how it works.

Product: _____

Scene 1	Scene 2	Scene 3	Scene 4	Scene 5

Name _____   Date _____

Review Vocabulary

A. Choose a word from the box that is an antonym of the underlined word or phrase.

vile	seldom	contrived
frail	elaborate	coincidence

1. The thief <u>thoughtlessly told</u> a story to explain his innocence. _____

2. An Internet browser with animation, virtual reality, sound, and music files is <u>simple</u>.

   _____

3. The story is about a colony of <u>strong</u> people on a distant planet. _____

4. Since e-mail was invented, people <u>often</u> write letters by hand. _____

5. A <u>pleasant</u> smell came out of the city's sewers. _____

6. It was a <u>plan</u> that we both went to the same movie at the same time. _____

B. Read the dialogue. Write a word from the box that BEST completes each sentence. Use the words in parentheses as clues.

nuzzled	depicted	elaborate	predict	coincidence
develop	seldom	reaction	devices	contrived

Abby: I love science fiction! I just saw a movie that _____ (showed) humans
   living on a distant planet. The settings were weird and fascinating. I could imagine myself
   using the futuristic _____ (machines) the characters used.

Lazaro: The settings aren't really weird. They're just the present in disguise. I think sci-fi writers take
   our current situations and use them to _____ (figure out possibilities)
   their ideas. They want people to go out and solve problems today.

Abby: What? That's not my _____ (response). When I see sci-fi movies, I
   feel entertained and amazed. Sci-fi writers like Jules Verne always _____
   (tell what will happen) the future.

Lazaro: What about H.G. Wells? He _____ (specifically created) a
   character that built a time machine. The story takes place centuries in the future. Wells was
   really criticizing his own society in England.

Abby: Well, I'll see for myself. You can find me at home _____ (put close)
   with my cat while I read *The Time Machine*.

Name _____   Date _____

Extend Vocabulary

A. Many English words come from the Latin word *dicere*, which means "say." Underline the Latin root *dict-* in the following words. Use the Latin roots in the box and your affixionary to write the definitions.

1. **contradict** _____

2. **dictate** _____

3. **dictionary** _____

4. **predict** _____

5. **dictator** _____

6. **benediction** _____

7. **verdict** _____

More Latin Roots

bene—good; well

contra—against

ver—true

B. Choose the BEST word from Part A to answer each question.

1. At the end of a trial, the judge tells the truth. What does everyone wait for her to say?

   _____

2. The magician looked into the crystal ball. He was about to tell something before it happened. What did the audience want him to do? _____

3. The dying chief told his tribe he wished them well in the future. What did he give them?

   _____

4. You speak, and I write what you say. What do you do? _____

5. One person controls everything in a certain country. What he says is law. What kind of leader is he?

   _____

6. A book says a lot about thousands of words. What kind of book is it? _____

7. Your friend says that sushi is delicious. "I know you will say something against that," she adds. What does she think you'll do? _____

Name _____ Date _____

Assess Comprehension and Vocabulary

A. Read the passage. Visualize images as you read descriptions in the passage. Make new predictions as you learn new information.

What do you predict buildings of the future need? One architect asked himself that question before he began to develop his plans. Dr. Ken Yeang knew that buildings must be tall because cities were getting more crowded. He also knew that tall buildings use a lot of energy, which could be harmful to the environment. What was his solution? He decided to design tall buildings that would not hurt the environment. Many of Yeang's buildings are designed for a tropical climate where it is seldom cold. He uses renewable resources like the sun, wind, and plants. Many of his buildings have plants that grow in spirals up the sides. The elaborate landscaping is not just pretty. It is useful too. Plants give off oxygen while cooling and shading the building. Fresh air blows through open windows and doors for ventilation. Sunroofs brighten the rooms with sunlight. By using the wind and sunlight, people use less energy for fans and lights. Yeang is designing more buildings. He plans for the energy for heat and electrical power to come from wind and the sun. Most people have a positive reaction to the skyscrapers he builds. Architecture organizations have honored him with awards.

B. Circle the letter of each correct answer.

1. What is the BEST definition of the word *develop*?
   A. declare that something will happen in the future
   B. work out the possibilities of something
   C. show something in a picture or by using words
   D. obviously planned or calculated; not spontaneous

2. What is a synonym for the word *reaction*?
   A. response
   B. prediction
   C. plan
   D. activate

3. What is the BEST definition of the word *predict*?
   A. declare that something will happen in the future
   B. work out the possibilities of something
   C. show something in a picture or by using words
   D. obviously planned or calculated; not spontaneous

4. What is an antonym for the word *seldom*?
   A. rarely
   B. frail
   C. often
   D. strangely

Name _____   Date _____

5. What is a synonym for the word *elaborate*?
    A. ordinary
    B. simple
    C. remarkable
    D. complicated

6. Choose the title that BEST fits the passage.
    A. The Life of an Architect
    B. Yeang's Skyscraper Solutions
    C. Tropical Landscaping in Skyscrapers
    D. Using Renewable Resources

7. What is the main idea of the passage?
    A. Skyscrapers of the future must be taller.
    B. Ken Yeang is an award-winning architect.
    C. Ken Yeang uses interesting landscape features.
    D. Ken Yeang's buildings are a good solution for the future.

8. Why are tall buildings harmful to the environment?
    A. It takes a long time to build them.
    B. They block the view of the sun.
    C. They use a lot of energy.
    D. A lot of people work inside them.

9. What resource does the passage NOT describe?
    A. sun
    B. wind
    C. plants
    D. oil

10. Why are renewable resources important to Ken Yeang?
    A. They are inexpensive and modern.
    B. They are good for the environment.
    C. They are easy to design.
    D. They are beautiful.

11. Why will other architects develop similar buildings for the future?
    A. More people need buildings, and the environment must be protected.
    B. Architects will imitate Ken Yeang's buildings because he has won awards.
    C. Energy for cars will be scarce, so people will live in the building where they work.
    D. Other architects will not design buildings that are similar.

12. What statement does NOT describe the plants around the buildings?
    A. pretty landscaping
    B. grow in spirals up the sides
    C. crops of ripe vegetables
    D. cool and shade the building

13. Which description does NOT describe a skyscraper that Ken Yeang builds?
    A. very tall with solid glass sides
    B. in a crowded city
    C. has green plants in many places
    D. lets in natural sunlight

Name _____ **Date** _____

14. What do you think Ken Yeang would say
is NOT important for designing buildings in
the future?

A. renewable resources

B. making smaller buildings

C. heat and electrical power

D. cooling and shading a building

15. Draw a picture or diagram of a building designed by Ken Yeang. Make sure you include and label at least three features described in the text.

Name _____ Date _____

Reteach

You can stop and visualize what you read. Underline the words that make pictures come to mind. After each numbered part, answer the question at the right.

The Future on Display

Companies show off their products at the International Consumer Electronics Show each year. What do you think of these new technologies?

1. Watch Phone

This watch might make you look like you are starring in a science fiction spy movie. It is both a watch and a phone. You can use it to text message, take photos and videos, and play music files.

2. MP3 Sunglasses

These sunglasses don't just look good. They are one of the newest ways to listen to music. They protect your eyes from the sun, look stylish, and let you answer phone calls and listen to your favorite music with attached earpieces.

3. Computerized Pen

This pen could make taking notes easier. A camera near the pen's tip records the notes. The computer in the pen knows the writer's handwriting. An audio recorder can record the lecture. The user can upload notes to a laptop.

4. Brain-Powered Game

You might think that telekinesis, the ability to move objects with mental power, is imaginary. Think again. A new game has been released that uses energy from the brain to move a ping-pong size ball through a series of hoops and tubes.

1. Do you think the watch phone will become popular? Explain.

_____

_____

_____

_____

2. What are two familiar things? How do they help you visualize MP3 sunglasses?

_____

_____

_____

_____

3. How could it be useful to record talking and writing?

_____

_____

_____

_____

4. Predict what the writer will say to finish the description. Hint: Reread the other descriptions.

_____

_____

_____

_____

Name _____ Date _____

WHO WAS JULES VERNE?

Jules Verne (1828–1905) was an imaginative science fiction writer who lived in France more than 100 years ago. Verne's exciting adventure stories were filled with memorable characters who went on wild rides in different parts of the world—on land, under the sea, and in the air. Some characters journeyed to the center of the earth. Others raced around the world by train, by boat, and on the back of an elephant. Throughout the years, millions of readers have been captivated by Verne's stories.

But, what made Jules Verne exceptional was that his stories contained inventions that hadn't yet been created. Known as the father of science fiction, Verne described appliances and devices—such as air conditioning, cars, and television—that would not become commonplace for 100 years or more. How did Verne predict these inventions? How did Verne anticipate the scientific discoveries of the future?

In the spirit of fiction writing, we "interviewed" Verne as an elderly man, to find out about his life, his works, and his methods.

Q: Some of your stories, such as *20,000 Leagues Under the Sea* and *Journey to the Center of the Earth*, contain scientific information in a range of fields. How did you know so much about astronomy, biology, physics, and oceanography?

A: I read several newspapers every day and took notes on what I read. Also, I went to libraries where I read books about geology, engineering, architecture, marine biology, and astronomy, depending on my interests at the time. Sometimes on afternoons when I wasn't writing, I visited shops and factories in my neighborhood to see how things were made. Overall, I used my imagination to project present-day scientific principles into the future.

Q: But for some fields like space travel, very little was known in your day. Yet, your books describe space travel as it would be developed years later. How did you do that?

A: I daydreamed a lot. Sometimes I wrote about something I wish existed, like a rocket ship. Keep in mind that my primary goal was to tell a gripping story. If I thought of an invention that would propel my story forward and made scientific sense, I incorporated it into the narrative. I had no way to know for sure if things really would develop that way. My job was to write an adventure story people would want to read.

Q: Did you find early success as a writer?

A: No, my early manuscripts were rejected.

Q: Did the publishers say why?

A: Yes, they said they were too scientific!

Name _____ Date _____

Q: Yet, you went on to become a highly successful author. What changed?

A: I met a publisher who read my first manuscript. He suggested I add some funny incidents to my story. He said I should change a sad ending to a happy one. I took his advice. He published my story, and readers loved it. Then readers wanted more. That's how my career as a science fiction author was launched.

Q: Your book *20,000 Leagues Under the Sea* was a huge success. What sparked your interest in writing about underwater travel?

A: As a child in France, my brother and I used to rent a boat during the summer and row along the river. I watched huge ships float down the Loire. I was small; the ships were large. I fantasized that I was the captain of one of those mammoth ships. Then my mind wandered even more. What was life like deep in the ocean? Were there scary sea monsters there that terrorized mammals and fish? What did those monsters eat? How long did they live? Could man-made submarines survive in the ocean depths? Those random thoughts formed the early ideas for the book.

Q: How did you learn to write fiction?

A: As a child, I read a lot, which I greatly enjoyed. When I became a man, I wrote books I would have liked to have read as a young adult. Early on, I wrote in all kinds of genres: stories, poems, songs, and plays. But, I was best at writing stories, so I stayed with that.

Q: What was your parents' reaction to you becoming a writer?

A: My father was furious. He wanted me to be a lawyer like him. My mother didn't object.

Q: You are still writing today, even as an elderly man. What are your writing habits?

A: I wake up before sunrise at about 5 a.m. and write until early afternoon. In the evening, before bedtime, I read scientific journals as well as fiction as preparation for work. Also, my dreams often give me ideas for new adventure stories. In the morning, I write down my dreams in case I want to use snippets in future books.

Q: Can you describe some scientific invention that we will see in the future?

A: *Moi?* I'll leave that task to today's science fiction writers. The future is theirs.

Q: Add your own question for Jules Verne:

_____

_____

_____

_____

A: Answer your question as Jules Verne would have.

_____

_____

_____

_____

Name _____   Date _____

Exploring Careers: Writer/Author

A. Answer the following questions about a career as a writer or author.

1. What do technical writers do?

   _____

   _____

2. What three things do editors do?

   _____

   _____

3. What are three activities a writer might do during the day?

   _____

   _____

4. What was the median annual salary for writers and authors in 2006?

   _____

5. Why is it sometimes important for writers to research in person? For example, a writer might interview others, visit a place, or experience something rather than just read about it.

   _____

   _____

   _____

B. Use the Internet to research other possible career choices in this field and complete the chart.	
Career	
Responsibilities	
Education Required	
Average Salary	
Is this a career you might pursue?	
Why or why not?	
Career	
Responsibilities	
Education Required	
Average Salary	
Is this a career you might pursue?	
Why or why not?	

Name _____   Date _____

Vocabulary

"The Cloning Revolution"

A. Rate your knowledge of each boldfaced word.

3 familiar
2 somewhat familiar
1 unknown word

☐ **typically** (adv) *how things usually are; generally*
Unless they are cloned, mammals *typically* have two parents.

☐ **deliberate** (adj) *planned or intended*
After years of thinking, he made a *deliberate* decision to clone a sheep.

☐ **replicate** (v) *make a copy of; duplicate*
She wanted to perfectly *replicate* her beloved dog that she missed.

☐ **intense** (adj) *involving or showing extreme effort*
The *intense* look on the scientist's face showed his concentration.

☐ **differentiate** (v) *show a difference between two things*
Ms. McKinney couldn't *differentiate* between the cloned puppies because they had the exact same DNA.

☐ **generated** (v) *produced; created*
All the trees at the tree farm were *generated* from a single tree.

B. Choose the boldfaced word from Part A that BEST answers each question.

1. Which word goes with "something you have made yourself"? _____

2. Which word would you use to say you will make a copy of the DVD? _____

3. Which word describes how it feels to take a difficult test? _____

4. Which word would you use to say you could tell twins apart? _____

5. Which word goes with "something you usually do"? _____

6. Which word goes with "making a decision on purpose"? _____

Name _____   Date _____

Word Building

A. The words *replicate* and *differentiate* end with *-ate*. This suffix means "make, cause, or act." Read the following verbs and their meanings.

accentuate	*make more noticeable*
compensate	*make payment or amends to*
duplicate	*make a copy*
retaliate	*act unpleasantly because someone has acted that way toward you*
proliferate	*cause to grow or spread rapidly*
regenerate	*cause to form again or replace*

B. Think about the meanings of the words in Part A and how you have heard each word used. Complete each sentence with a word from the list.

1. She was upset that her sister broke her camera, so she decided to _____ by breaking her sister's TV.

2. Some women use cosmetics to _____ their eyes and lips.

3. Sea stars and earthworms are two animals that are able to _____ their own damaged body parts.

4. At restaurants, diners usually _____ the waitstaff with a tip.

5. Computer viruses _____ rapidly if they are not stopped by antivirus software.

6. Since Dolly the sheep was cloned, other scientists have tried to _____ the same process for pets.

C. Choose two words from the list in Part A that apply to your own life. Give an example of how each word relates to your life.

Word	How It Relates to My Life
1. _____	_____
2. _____	_____

Name _____   Date _____

Cause and Effect

A. Read the effects and determine each cause.

1. _____

    Effect 1: stillbirth
    Effect 2: premature death
    Effect 3: illness

2. _____

    Effect 1: She was devastated.
    Effect 2: She wanted to keep the dog's memory alive.
    Effect 3: She had the dog cloned.

B. Complete the graphic organizer to show multiple effects of each cause. Remember that a cause is what happens and an effect is the result.

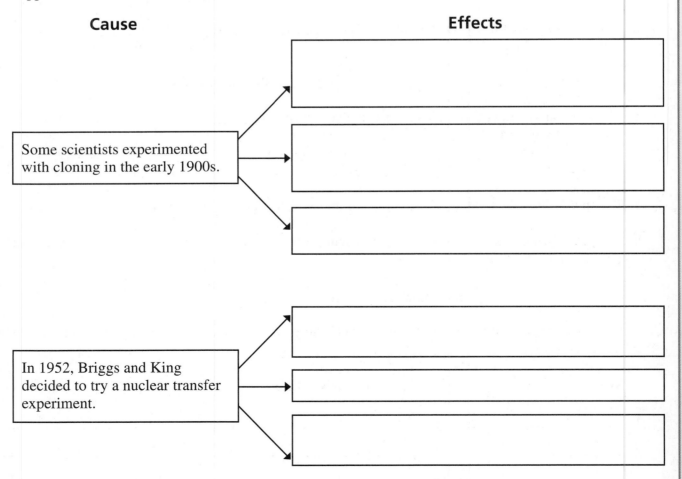

Cause

Effects

Some scientists experimented with cloning in the early 1900s.

In 1952, Briggs and King decided to try a nuclear transfer experiment.

Name _____   Date _____

Write in Response to Reading

A. Create a timeline of cloning milestones from "The Cloning Revolution." Include milestones from 1902 to the present.

1902: _____
_____

1928: _____
_____

1952: _____

1962: _____

1996: _____

2008: _____

B. People have strong opinions about the ethics of human cloning. Read the following quote from the passage, then write your opinion about human cloning. Use information in the passage and your own experience to support your opinion.

Despite this controversy, researchers went on to clone other animals including horses, mules, bulls, goats, pigs, rabbits, and cats. What or who would be next?

I think human cloning _____
_____
_____
_____
_____
_____
_____
_____
_____
_____
_____
_____
_____
_____
_____

Name _____ **Date** _____

Vocabulary

"Microchipping Humans"

A. Put a check mark in each row to indicate how well you know each boldfaced word.

	Know This Word	Have Seen This Word	Don't Know This Word
convenience (n) *something that is useful and easy to use* GPS is a modern *convenience* that helps us travel.			
debate (v) *discuss something* People in government often *debate* issues.			
conform (v) *act in an expected way* Governments expect their people to *conform* to rules.			
standards (n) *rules or models used to judge how good something is* The government sets *standards* on food quality.			
cautious (adj) *tries to avoid mistakes or danger* Vets are *cautious* when they insert microchips in pets because they don't want to hurt them.			
regulates (v) *controls or manages* In *1984*, Big Brother *regulates* the actions of the people through fear.			

B. Choose the boldfaced word from Part A that BEST completes each sentence.

1. A great _____ for most teens today is text messaging instead of calling.

2. My English teacher uses specific _____ when grading essays and stories.

3. Students know they must _____ to school rules.

4. The government _____ the way food and drugs are manufactured.

5. Internet shoppers should be _____ about sharing personal information.

6. Teens often _____ the fairness of laws related to driving cars.

Name _____   Date _____

Word Building

A. Many words have Greek or Latin roots. The Latin root *form* means "shape, figure, or appearance." In English, words with *form* can be adjectives or verbs. Read the following words.

biform (adj)	**uniform** (adj)	**reform** (v)
formless (adj)	**deform** (v)	**transform** (v)

B. Read the affixes and their meanings. Think of words you already know with each affix. Write those words next to each of the following affixes.

bi-   two   _____   *de-*   opposite of _____

re-   again   _____   *trans-* change   _____

uni- same as; one _____   *-less* without   _____

C. The prefixes are clues to the meanings of the words in Part A. Use the prefix and root to determine the correct word for each meaning.

1. change shape or form _____

2. put out of normal form or shape _____

3. form or shape again _____

4. without shape _____

5. have the same, or identical, form or appearance _____

6. have two shapes or forms _____

D. Circle the correct word to complete each sentence.

1. Some people want to (reform, uniform) current laws to protect personal privacy.

2. The officers looked (biform, uniform) in their blue police gear.

3. Do you think microchip technology will (transform, perform) how people make purchases in the future?

4. Inserting a microchip under the skin will not (perform, deform) your pet.

5. Do you think scientists will be able to create (platform, biform) creatures that are half human and half animal?

6. I worked with the (uniform, formless) blob of clay to make a vase.

Name _____   Date _____

Ask Questions

Generate a question for each level as you read, then find the answer. Begin with the first level at the bottom of the chart.

	Generate a Question	Find the Answer	
Top Level My Opinion			
Fifth Level Hypothesize	What would happen if . . .		
Fourth Level Compare/ Contrast		The benefits include identifying lost children, accessing medical records for ill people, and shopping with ease. The negative effects include the potential for hacking, the loss of privacy, and loss of freedom.	
Third Level Relate to My Life	How will microchips affect . . .		
Second Level Summarize			
Facts	What is the purpose of microchipping people or pets?		

Name _____ **Date** _____

Write in Response to Reading

Imagine that you work for a human microchip company. The president has given you the opportunity to make a televised speech to the nation. What would you say to persuade people to get a microchip?

_____

_____

_____

_____

_____

_____

_____

_____

_____

_____

_____

_____

_____

_____

_____

_____

_____

_____

_____

_____

_____

_____

_____

_____

_____

_____

_____

_____

Name _____ Date _____

Review Vocabulary

A. For each vocabulary word, write either *S* for a synonym or *A* for an antonym.

deliberate	_____ intended	_____ accidental	_____ planned
intense	_____ mild	_____ extreme	_____ strong
conform	_____ obey	_____ rebel	_____ follow
standards	_____ rules	_____ models	_____ guidelines
cautious	_____ safe	_____ reckless	_____ careful
typically	_____ usually	_____ rarely	_____ normally

B. Write a word from the box that BEST completes each sentence. Use the words in parentheses as clues.

convenience	**debate**	**generated**
differentiate	**replicate**	**regulates**

1. It was nearly impossible to _____ (tell the difference between) the identical twins.

2. The researchers wanted to _____ (copy) the strongest and healthiest horses.

3. Scientists have _____ (produced) clones of sheep, pigs, goats, and horses.

4. The government _____ (controls) spending on genetic research.

5. Cell phones are a modern _____ (easy thing to use) that make communication easier.

6. Many concerned people _____ (discuss) the issue of using microchips in humans.

C. Read each question, then write the answer on the line.

1. What do you *typically* do on the weekend?

   _____

   _____

2. Name two things that are a *convenience* to you.

   _____

   _____

Name _____   Date _____

Extend Vocabulary

A. Many words have Greek or Latin roots. The Greek word *genos* and the Latin word *genus* mean "race, people, kind, and offspring." Each of the following words contains the root *gen*. Read the words and their meanings. Notice how the English words still contain the meanings of the Greek and Latin words.

genealogy (n)	*a line of family descent traced from an ancestor*
generation (n)	*a set of people who are born and living at the same time*
genetic (adj)	*relating to genes, heredity, or inheritance*
gender (n)	*male or female*
generic (adj)	*general; belonging to no specific group or people*

B. Think about the meanings of the words in Part A and how you have heard each word used. Complete each sentence with a word from the list.

1. The clones have the exact same _____ traits.

2. The bathrooms were separated according to _____.

3. The bottles of brand-name soda were more expensive than the _____ bottles.

4. Marie traced her _____ back to her great-great-grandparents.

5. Our current _____ enjoys faster and easier technology than ever before.

C. Circle the correct word in each sentence.

1. Teams of biologists have been working on cures for (genetic, generic) diseases.

2. Each of the cloned puppies is exactly identical to the previous (genealogy, generation).

3. The new litter of puppies contained an equal number from each (generation, gender).

4. He has studied his mom's (genealogy, gender) to find out if twins existed in past families.

5. His (genealogy, generic) speech was not intended for any specific group.

Name _____ Date _____

Assess Comprehension and Vocabulary

A. Read the passage. Notice causes and effects in the text.

> Androids, or human-looking robots, might seem like something only from science fiction movies. You might be surprised to find out that Japanese scientists already have created a robot that appears very human. Her name is Repliee Q1Expo, and she resembles a Japanese woman. Professor Hiroshi Ishiguro has generated many robots before, but Repliee Q1Expo looks the most human. She has realistic hair. Her skin is flexible silicon rather than hard plastic. She even moves like a human being. Her eyelids flutter, and she also can appear to breathe. A computer programmed her motion to replicate human motions. Repliee Q1Expo actually can interact with people. Professor Ishiguro says people sometimes forget they are interacting with an android and not a woman. Perhaps someday, scientists will create an android so real that it will be hard to differentiate between androids and humans.

B. Circle the letter of each correct answer.

1. Which word BEST replaces *generated* in the following sentence?
   Professor Hiroshi Ishiguro has _____ many robots before.
   A. destroyed
   B. introduced
   C. produced
   D. discovered

2. What is a synonym for the word *replicate*?
   A. distinguish
   B. copy
   C. react
   D. follow

3. What word describes two things that are difficult to *differentiate*?
   A. familiar
   B. understandable
   C. different
   D. identical

4. What is the main idea of this passage?
   A. Androids could take over the world.
   B. Repliee Q1Expo can interact with people.
   C. Repliee Q1Expo is like a real human in many ways.
   D. Robots could fool us into thinking they are human.

Name _____   Date _____

5. Why will it soon be difficult to differentiate between androids and humans?
   A. Humans will become more robotic.
   B. Androids will look so real.
   C. People will begin to die.
   D. Androids will have silicon hair.

6. What is probably the reason Repliee Q1Expo looks like a Japanese woman?
   A. She was created by Japanese scientists.
   B. She is the first realistic robot.
   C. She was created for a family in Tokyo.
   D. She was created in Germany.

7. People think android Repliee Q1Expo is like a human. Which of the following is NOT a cause?
   A. She appears to breathe.
   B. She has realistic hair.
   C. Her eyelids flutter.
   D. She has a computer inside her.

8. People can interact with Repliee Q1Expo. What is the effect?
   A. Her movements replicate human motions.
   B. People forget that she is not a human.
   C. It is hard to differentiate humans from robots.
   D. Japanese scientists have created an android.

9. What would be a good title for this passage?
   A. Androids in Our Future
   B. Androids in Science Fiction
   C. Meet Repliee Q1Expo
   D. Programming Robots

Name _____ Date _____

C. Read the passage. Notice causes and their effects in the text. Remember, you may have to infer a cause or effect if the text does not state it directly.

> You are probably already aware that many plants and animals are extinct or endangered. Many species are threatened because of pollution, hunting, and other human causes. That's why many scientific researchers are busy making a deliberate attempt to collect genetic samples of thousands of plants and animals. The samples are stored in frozen vaults called gene banks. These storage facilities are an intense effort to save species from dying out. Scientists hope that someday we might be able to make clones of these plants and animals. Some of these species are plants that grow food. In case of a future famine, this will be a back-up supply. Hopefully, such a crisis will never happen.

D. Circle the letter of each correct answer.

10. What is a synonym for the word *deliberate*?
    A. excessive
    B. needed
    C. planned
    D. tragic

11. What is an antonym for the word *intense*?
    A. mild
    B. extreme
    C. scientific
    D. severe

12. What is the topic of the passage?
    A. pollution
    B. gene banks
    C. famines
    D. cloning

13. Plants and animals have become extinct or endangered. What is a cause?
    A. People pollute and hunt.
    B. People starve during famines.
    C. Genetic samples are in storage.
    D. Scientists generate clones.

14. What would be a good title for this passage?
    A. Saving the Future from Famine
    B. Storing Life-Forms in a Gene Bank
    C. Species on the Endangered List
    D. Extinct Animals and What Happened

15. Scientists might make clones with the stored plant and animal genetic samples. What is the effect?

_____

_____

Name _____   Date _____

Reteach

Read the following passage. Notice causes and effects in the passage. Find signal words or phrases, such as *so, because, since, reason, made,* and *as a result*. Answer the questions for each portion of the passage. Remember that a **cause** is why something happened and an **effect** is what happened.

Renewable Energy Means Clean Energy

For many decades, we have made electricity for our homes by burning coal. We also have run our vehicles on gasoline and oil. Burning coal and oil puts several pollutants into the air. Those pollutants have caused environmental harm, such as smog, acid rain, and global warming. Resources like coal and oil also eventually will become depleted, or run out. Concerned scientists are developing ways to use renewable sources of energy. Renewable means that the energy source will not run out. These sources are found naturally in our environment. Renewable sources include water, sunlight, wind, and heat from inside the earth.

Hydropower

Hydropower is a way of converting the energy of falling water into electricity. The power of water flowing through a dam turns a turbine, which makes a generator turn. These mechanisms create electricity that a transformer transmits to power lines.

1. What signal words or phrases did you find in the passage?

   _____

   _____

   _____

2. Read the first paragraph.
   Cause: burning _____

   _____

   Effect: The air is polluted.

   Cause: Air pollution
   Effects: harm to the _____

   _____

   _____

   _____

3. Read about hydropower.
   Cause: Water _____

   _____

   Effect: The mechanisms in a dam turn, which creates electricity.

Name _____   Date _____

Solar Energy

Solar panels convert the sun's energy into electricity. When light hits a solar cell, it is absorbed into the material. As a result, the light is broken down into electrons, its smallest particles. The resulting flow of electrons is a current of electricity.

Wind Energy

Just like a hydropower dam, the turning motion of windmills results in energy generation. Wind causes the blades of the wind-electric turbine to turn. The generator makes that rotational energy into electricity.

Geothermal Energy

Geothermal energy can replace traditional heating and air conditioning systems. The earth has a steady temperature. By using the temperatures underground, we can heat and cool homes and other buildings. Temperatures are rather cool in the shallow ground near the earth's surface. Deeper in the earth, there is hot rock, water, and steam.

4. Read about solar energy.
   Cause: The light _____
   _____

   Effect: The light breaks down into electrons.

5. Read about wind energy.
   Cause: Wind blows past the wind-electric turbine.

   Effects: The blades _____
   _____
   _____

6. Read about geothermal energy.
   Cause: There are cool areas and hot areas underground.

   Effect: We can _____
   _____
   _____

7. What effect do all these resources have in common?

   _____
   _____

Name _____ Date _____

Is a Microchip Right for Your Pet?

Like other pet owners, you care greatly about the health and safety of your cat or dog. So, what would you do if your animal got lost—in your neighborhood, on a family vacation, or during a storm?

Nowadays, this is a problem facing many loving pet owners. Fortunately, there is a way to help reunite a lost pet with its family. The solution? Ask your veterinarian to implant a microchip in your animal.

What is a microchip?

A microchip is a small electronic transistor placed under the animal's skin. The size of a grain of rice, the microchip gives off a radio signal with electronic information.

If your pet is found by an animal shelter, the veterinarian there uses a scanner to read your pet's ID number from the microchip. Then the vet consults a computer where he or she finds your contact information from a national registry.

What are the advantages of inserting a microchip in my pet?

Many pet owners say that the microchip gives them peace of mind. If their pet gets lost or stolen, the microchip helps to get their pet back home.

How is the microchip implanted?

The veterinarian uses a needle to implant the microchip. The needle is slightly larger than that used to give your pet a vaccination.

Name _____   Date _____

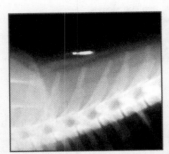

My cat has an ID tag and my dog has a collar. Is that enough?
An ID tag or collar can be torn off or removed. But a microchip, placed under the skin, cannot be removed.

Will implanting a microchip hurt my pet?
No, your pet may feel a slight pinch or nothing at all. The veterinarian implants the chip in the fleshy part of your animal between its shoulder blades where it doesn't hurt.

Will my pet have an allergic reaction?
The microchip is stationary. Your pet will not have an allergic reaction.

Will my pet be awake when the microchip is implanted?
Yes, the experience is similar to your pet being awake when getting a vaccination shot.

Does a microchip wear out?
A microchip lasts the lifetime of your pet.

I have many pets: two cats, a dog, a bird, and a snake. Can all my animals get a microchip?
Yes, a microchip can be implanted in cats, dogs, birds, reptiles, even horses!

How much does it cost?
The cost of implanting a microchip is less than $40. At some clinics and shelters, it is free.

Name _____   Date _____

Exploring Careers: Embryologist

A. Answer the following questions about a career as an embryologist.

1. What are three types of embryologists?

   _____

   _____

2. What are four places where an embryologist might work?

   _____

3. What education does an embryologist need?

   _____

   _____

4. What interests, skills, or abilities make an embryologist successful?

   _____

   _____

   _____

5. How do you think an embryologist's work might be rewarding?

   _____

   _____

   _____

   _____

B. Use the Internet to research other possible career choices in this field and complete the chart.	
Career	
Responsibilities	
Education Required	
Average Salary	
Is this a career you might pursue?	
Why or why not?	
Career	
Responsibilities	
Education Required	
Average Salary	
Is this a career you might pursue?	
Why or why not?	

Name _____ Date _____

A. Organize Your Ideas

Fashionistas

-
-
-

Which fashions are really new, and which have been recycled from previous generations?

-
-
-

What are the pros and cons of school uniforms?

-
-
-

How does brand influence the clothes you purchase?

-
-
-

What else would you like to know about fashion?

_____

_____

B. The Big Picture

Different passages give you different ideas. Write notes for each passage. Combine ideas from each passage to get the big picture, or what's important.

"Boomerang Fashion"
_____
_____
_____
_____
_____

"Are You What You Wear?"
_____
_____
_____
_____
_____

The Big Picture: What's important?
_____
_____
_____
_____

"Uniforms: Just Right or All Wrong?"
_____
_____
_____
_____

"In the Public Eye"
_____
_____
_____
_____

C. Expedition Dictionary

You will read the following vocabulary words throughout the Expedition. As you learn the words, use them as often as possible in your oral and written language.

"Boomerang Fashion"

fashion	(n) *the popular or up-to-date way of dressing, speaking, or behaving; the style*
synthetic	(adj) *something man-made or artificial; not found in nature*
coordinate	(v) *work well together*
practical	(adj) *useful and sensible*
modern	(adj) *having to do with the latest styles, methods, or ideas; up-to-date*

"Are You What You Wear?"

judgment	(n) *a strong opinion*
behavior	(n) *the way someone acts*
accurate	(adj) *correct; without mistakes or errors*
discriminate	(v) *make a difference in treatment on a basis other than individual merit*
portray	(v) *make a picture or mental image of*

"Uniforms: Just Right or All Wrong?"

personal	(adj) *one's own; private or individual*
control	(v) *be in charge of; direct*
conservative	(adj) *traditional or modest*
focus	(v) *fix attention on something*
individual	(n) *a single being or thing*

"In the Public Eye"

goods	(n) *things that can be bought or sold; products*
loyal	(adj) *faithful to someone or something*
bias	(v) *cause someone's way of thinking to change to be in favor of or against*
manufacture	(v) *make products in large amounts*
consumers	(n) *people who buy products or services; customers*

Dictionary Challenge

Write a fashion-themed story or description of a garment using as many of the vocabulary words as possible.

Name _____   Date _____

Vocabulary

"Boomerang Fashion"

A. Rate your knowledge of each boldfaced word.

3 familiar
2 somewhat familiar
1 unknown word

fashion (n) *the popular or up-to-date way of dressing, speaking, or behaving; the style*
The clothing store on the corner has the newest *fashion*.

synthetic (adj) *something man-made or artificial; not found in nature*
Cotton is a natural fiber; nylon is *synthetic*.

coordinate (v) *work well together*
Tennis shoes don't *coordinate* with an evening gown.

practical (adj) *useful and sensible*
Pants without pockets are not very *practical*.

modern (adj) *having to do with the latest styles, methods, or ideas; up-to-date*
Our new furniture is very *modern*.

B. Choose the ending that BEST completes each sentence.

as much as cotton and wool ones	**reasons and to make a fashion statement too**
an outfit	**styles are featured in this magazine**
the clothes may cost more	

1. When you buy the latest **fashion,** _____.

2. Ads for all the **modern** _____.

3. I don't like the feel of **synthetic** fabrics _____.

4. You choose colors, styles, and accessories when you **coordinate** _____.

5. People use purses for **practical** _____.

Name _____   Date _____

Inference

"Boomerang Fashion"

A. Cut out pictures of people from magazines that show different fashions. Arrange and glue them into the box to show different activities based on the fashion or clothing style. Draw accessories such as hats or shoes as necessary.

B. Work with a partner to make inferences about each other's pictures. Write your inferences on your partner's paper on the lines provided. Discuss whether the inferences make sense or not.

_____

_____

_____

_____

Name _____   Date _____

Word Building

A. The prefix *syn-* means "together." Read the following words and definitions. Think about how each meaning relates to the idea of "together."

Words	Definitions
synthetic (adj)	*something man-made or artificial; not found in nature*
synthesis (n)	*the combining of two or more things to make something new*
synchronize (v)	*cause to happen at the same time*
syntax (n)	*the way words are put together to make sentences*
syndrome (n)	*a group of symptoms that happen together*

B. Choose the word from Part A that BEST completes each sentence.

1. Weakness and loss of appetite are sometimes part of a serious medical _____.

2. If you say, "Give you me a pencil," you are using incorrect _____.

3. The labels on clothing tell if the fabric is made of natural or _____ fibers.

4. The fashion model planned to _____ her movements with the background music as she walked down the runway.

5. Ray created a casual clothing design, which was a _____ of formal clothing and athletic wear.

C. Choose two words from Part A and write a sentence with each word.

1. _____

   _____

2. _____

   _____

Name _____   Date _____

Inference

Complete the statements to make inferences about "Boomerang Fashion."

What Is in the Text	What I Already Know	What I Infer
Bell-bottom pants were part of the navy uniform in the early 1800s.		Modern navy uniforms are
Some people said certain fashions caused bad behavior.		Fashions have a strong influence on people. They can cause
an illustration of the woman in a corset on page 180		People today would not wear this fashion because
The fashion industry dictates changing and recycling trends. (*Dictates* means "orders" or "commands" the trends.)		The fashion business's influence on me is
With ever-changing fashion trends, a person might wonder why people like to buy the latest fashion.		

Name _____   Date _____

Write in Response to Reading

Draw your idea of a shirt that may become an exciting new fashion. Write a character sketch, or description, of a person—famous or unknown—who feels that your new style expresses who he or she is.

Illustration	Character Sketch

Name _____ Date _____

Vocabulary

"Are You What You Wear?"

A. Put a check mark in each row to indicate how well you know each boldfaced word.

	Know This Word	Have Seen This Word	Don't Know This Word
judgment (n) *a strong opinion* When I saw the small size of the barking dog, I formed the *judgment* that I was safe.			
behavior (n) *the way someone acts* Talking on your cell phone during a movie is considered impolite *behavior.*			
accurate (adj) *correct; without mistakes or errors* Claims that teenagers are lazy and rude are not *accurate.*			
discriminate (v) *make a difference in treatment on a basis other than individual merit* It isn't fair to *discriminate* against people who are different from you.			
portray (v) *make a picture or mental image of* In my description, I tried to *portray* what really happened.			

B. Complete each sentence with the correct vocabulary word from Part A.

1. Workers in a mall store called security officers because a customer's _____ was violent.

2. The sales associate checked the price of each item I bought to make sure the total was

   _____.

3. Does this store _____ against any type of person who applies for a job?

4. When I saw Allie wearing certain clothes, I made a quick _____ that she was exactly like me.

5. The director of the play told me to _____ the monster as a creature with human emotions.

Name _____ Date _____

Word Building

A. Some suffixes change a word's part of speech. The suffix *-ment* can change some verbs into nouns. Read the words and their definitions.

Verbs	
amuse	*cause to smile or laugh*
judge	*form an opinion*
treat	*present or represent in a certain way*
amaze	*cause to feel great surprise or wonder*
require	*have need for; need*
develop	*grow or expand*

+ -ment

Nouns	
amusement	*condition of being amused or entertained*
judgment	*an opinion*
treatment	*techniques or actions applied to a specific thing or situation*
amazement	*great surprise or wonder*
requirement	*something needed*
development	*growth or expansion*

B. Choose a word from the lists in Part A that BEST completes each sentence.

1. The ability to sketch ideas is one _____ for the designer position.

2. It was hard to _____ which design was the best. I liked them all.

3. The fashion designer's _____ of lace on her dresses started a new style.

4. I watched in _____ as the models strutted down the runway in my designs.

5. Many designers _____ their style over a long period of time.

6. She hid her look of _____ when the model's hat slipped over her eyes.

7. The _____ of the designer's success did not happen overnight.

8. The designer wanted to shock and _____ the judges at the fashion show.

9. The fashion show organizers made the _____ that it was a success.

10. The model tried to _____ herself during the photo shoot by making jokes.

11. At this fine clothing shop, the customers _____ the best service.

12. A designer might _____ T-shirts differently by adding leather to the sleeve.

Name _____ Date _____

Inference

Use the chart headings and the prompts in the first column as steps to making inferences. Your inference must make sense with what you read in "Are You What You Wear?" and what you know.

What Is in the Text	What I Already Know	What I Infer
This is what the older generation thinks about fashion:		
This happens when people profile others:		
This happens when stores profile customers or employees:		
Profiling can have consequences:		

Name _____   Date _____

Write in Response to Reading

A. Have you ever been profiled? Write a description of the experience in the boxes. Include descriptive details about your appearance and behavior. What do you think the person or group reacted to when profiling you?

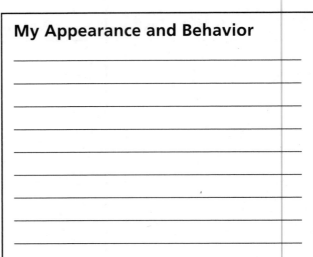

What Happened

_____
_____
_____
_____
_____
_____
_____
_____

My Appearance and Behavior

_____
_____
_____
_____
_____
_____
_____
_____

B. Write what you would say to the person or group to explain who you really are and why the judgment was wrong.

Who I Really Am

_____
_____
_____
_____
_____

C. Read each of the following questions, then write your answers on the lines.

1. How could you change your appearance and behavior to change someone's ideas about you?

_____
_____

2. Should you change your appearance and behavior to change the person's ideas? Explain.

_____
_____

Name _____ Date _____

Review Vocabulary

A. For each underlined word or phrase, write a synonym. Choose your answers from the words in the box.

accurate	discriminate	fashion	judgment	portray
practical	synthetic	coordinate	modern	behavior

1. Will the <u>current</u> styles of today look old-fashioned to your children? _____

2. Beth likes movies that <u>show</u> scenes with clothing styles of the past. _____

3. Your clothing may influence another person's <u>evaluation</u> of who you are. _____

4. Julian thinks that jeans and T-shirts are the most <u>sensible</u> clothing for school. _____

5. The 1980s-style suit that Urika made had <u>exact</u> details, such as large shoulder pads.

   _____

6. Some people <u>show prejudice</u> against people who wear certain clothing styles. _____

B. Read the dialogue. Write a word from the box in Part A that BEST completes each sentence. Use the words in parentheses as clues.

Akira: Let's see the gorgeous colors and fabrics in the new store. I'm excited about organic

_____ (style; way of dressing)!

Laura: Are organic clothes _____ (useful; sensible), or will they fall apart

right away? What are they made from? Corn husks?

Akira: They're as strong as any other clothes. But, the fabrics are natural, not _____

(man-made; not found in nature). You know, like cotton not corn.

Laura: I'll bet the clothes are old-fashioned and not _____ (up-to-date).

Akira: That's not _____ (correct) at all! The styles are trendy and will

_____ (match, work well together) with everything you have.

Laura: Yes, they do _____ (make a mental image of) you as an organic

fashionista. But, why else would you buy these clothes?

Akira: Think about how fabric is made. Organic fabrics are made without using harmful

chemicals in farming, softening, and coloring. Consumers should use good

_____ (ability to make decisions) and buy them to help the

environment.

Laura: Now I understand. My _____ (the way someone acts) as a consumer

affects the environment. Let's give that store a try!

Name _____ Date _____

Extend Vocabulary

A. Read the following words and definitions that use the prefixes *co-*, *con-*, *contro-*, and *contra-*.

Prefix	Words	Definitions
co- *together; with*	**coordinate** (v)	*match; fit well together*
	cooperation (n)	*helping; working together*
	correspond (v)	*be similar; comparable with*
con- *together; with*	**conversation** (n)	*dialogue; talking together*
	contribute (v)	*play a significant part with others*
contro-, contra- *against; opposite*	**controversy** (n)	*an issue that causes disagreement*
	contradict (v)	*state the opposite*
	contrary (adj)	*opposite in meaning or opinion*
	contrast (v)	*be strikingly different*

B. Complete each sentence with one of the words from Part A.

1. The issue of school uniforms is a major _____ at my school.

2. Alaina and Marta decided to _____ their help to make costumes for the school play.

3. Bell-bottom pants of the 1970s _____ to the bell-bottoms from old navy uniforms.

4. Clothing styles have changed greatly over time. Fashions from 100 years ago _____ with the current trends.

5. The designer created a line of clothing and accessories that girls could _____ into many outfits.

C. Are you what you wear? Use at least two words from Part A in your answer.

_____

_____

Name _____   Date _____

Assess Comprehension and Vocabulary

A. Read the following passage.

Organic and Fair-Trade Clothing

In the world of fashion, people are beginning to look for organic and fair-trade labels in clothing. Organic clothes are made without using harmful chemicals. Farmers don't use chemicals while growing the fibers. Manufacturers don't use them when they make the clothes. Fibers like cotton, hemp, and linen start as plants on farms. Many modern farmers use chemicals to kill bugs or make the plants grow bigger. That might seem like a practical way of farming, but it harms the environment. The chemicals get into the ground and water and may cause illness or death in plants, animals, and people. The process of making synthetic fabrics requires harmful chemicals. Some chemicals are bleaches and dyes used to color the newly woven cloth. Some are softeners that relax the stiff synthetic material. Organic clothes are made of only natural fibers. The organic clothing makers dye their fabric with vegetables, plants, and roots.

Fair-trade clothing is sold at a price that gives the workers enough money to take care of themselves and their families. Fair-trade agreements do not discriminate against workers in poor countries. The fair-trade workers are not forced to work extremely long days, so they are not overworked. They are paid fairly and work in safe, clean conditions.

B. Circle the letter of each correct answer.

1. What is a synonym for the word *fashion*?
   A. style
   B. modern
   C. trendy
   D. action

2. What is an antonym for the word *modern*?
   A. current
   B. up-to-date
   C. present
   D. old-fashioned

3. What is an antonym for the word *practical*?
   A. useful
   B. sensible
   C. useless
   D. reasonable

4. What is the BEST definition of the word *synthetic*?
   A. artificial; man-made; not found in nature
   B. trendy; fashionable; stylish
   C. good or proper virtue
   D. natural; grown on a farm

Name _____   Date _____

5. What is NOT an example of the word *discriminate*?

   A. treat unfairly

   B. be biased against

   C. be prejudiced

   D. have an argument

6. What would be another good title for the passage?

   A. How to Dye Fabric

   B. Fair and Safe Clothing

   C. In Style, Out of Style

   D. The New Organic Farm

7. What is the topic of this passage?

   A. shopping for clothing

   B. clothes that are better for workers and the environment

   C. farming cotton for clothing fabric

   D. chemicals in U.S. landfills

8. What is a farming practice that harms the environment?

   A. working long hours in factories

   B. dumping into landfills

   C. using chemicals in the soil

   D. using chemical dyes and bleaches

9. What is fair about fair-trade agreements?

   A. Workers are paid a living wage.

   B. Workers are not overworked.

   C. The work conditions are clean and safe.

   D. All of the above are true.

10. What item is used in making organic clothing?

    A. bug spray

    B. vegetable dye

    C. softeners

    D. bleach

11. Complete the statement about the cost of organically made clothes compared with synthetic clothes. Choose the inference that makes the BEST sense.
    Organically made clothes are . . .

    A. more expensive because not many farmers are using organic methods.

    B. more expensive because rich people like organic clothes and can afford them.

    C. less expensive because organic farmers are not interested in making money.

    D. less expensive because organic clothes are not as beautiful as synthetic clothes.

12. From the last two sentences in the passage, what would you infer about jobs for clothing workers who have a fair-trade agreement?

    A. Most workers dislike these jobs.

    B. Workers have more accidents at these jobs.

    C. Workers without fair-trade agreements might be overworked and underpaid.

    D. More of these jobs exist because more fair-trade companies are common.

Name _____   Date _____

13. What is the main reason to support organic clothing?

   A. Organic clothing is the current trend.

   B. Organic clothing comes in nice colors and fabrics.

   C. Organic clothing is made in a way that does not harm the environment.

   D. Organic clothing will go out of style unless everyone starts to buy it.

14. What could you infer about the plants on organic farms?

   A. They taste better than non-organic plants.

   B. Farmers use chemical sprays to kill bugs on the plants.

   C. Farmers have to find a safe way to kill bugs that eat the plants.

   D. They grow larger than plants on other farms that are not organic.

15. Which details from the passage helped you make the inference in the last question?

   _____

   _____

   _____

   _____

   _____

   _____

   _____

Name _____   Date _____

Reteach

A. Read the following passage.

Jarrett Patterson, Founder of Kids Closet

What can you do with a shirt that looks like new, but you don't wear anymore? Where can you get a new outfit if you can't afford to buy it? One student aimed to answer those questions for young people in Hudson, Michigan. Jarrett Patterson noticed many classmates and children at neighborhood schools who couldn't afford clothes. He developed a way to help, and the idea turned into Kids Closet. Jarrett contacts teachers to find students who might need clothing. At the same time, he collects donations of gently used clothing. When teachers e-mail Jarrett about special clothing requests, he goes through the donated clothing and fulfills those requests. The teachers pick up the clothes and deliver them to the student. Only Jarrett and the teachers know the students' names. Will some of your clothes appear in another kid's closet?

B. Use what you already know to answer the questions.

1. What can you do with your old clothes you don't wear anymore?

   _____

2. Where can you get a new outfit if you can't afford to buy new clothes?

   _____

C. Use details in the passage to answer the questions.

1. Who helps Jarrett give clothing to students who need them?

   _____

2. Which kids does Kids Closet benefit?

   _____

3. How do the teachers notify Jarrett of clothing requests?

   _____

Name _____   Date _____

D. You will not find the answers for the following questions stated directly in the passage. Make inferences by combining the details from the passage and what you already know.

1. Where do the clothing donations come from?

    I read that _____.

    I already know that _____.

    So, I make the inference that _____

    _____.

2. Why do Jarrett and the teachers not reveal the names of students who receive donated clothes?

    I read that _____.

    I already know that _____.

    So, I make the inference that _____

    _____.

3. What does Kids Closet need to be a successful program that will continue to help provide clothing for young people?

    I read that _____

    _____.

    I already know that _____

    _____

    _____.

    So, I make the inference that _____

    _____

    _____

    _____

    _____

    _____

Name _____ Date _____

Real World—Garment Label

As you read the following garment label, mark the text:

- Put a box around the fiber content.
- Put a star by the name of the country where the clothing was made
- Underline the name of the country where the fiber was grown or made.
- Why should the garment be washed alone the first time? Highlight this information.
- Circle when you add the fabric softener to the wash.

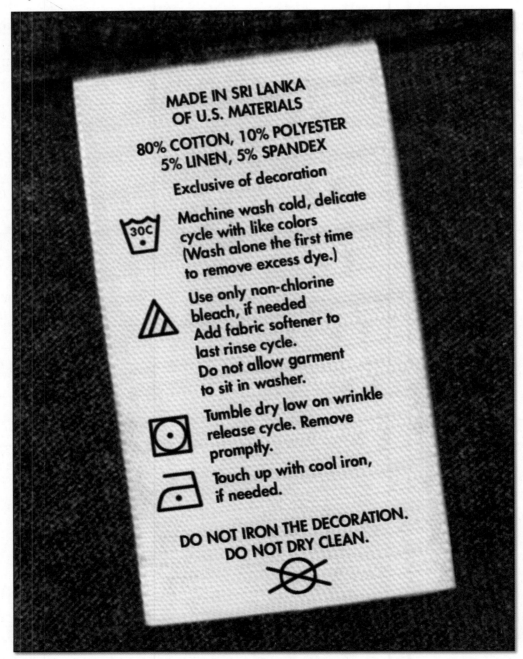

MADE IN SRI LANKA
OF U.S. MATERIALS
80% COTTON, 10% POLYESTER
5% LINEN, 5% SPANDEX
Exclusive of decoration

30C Machine wash cold, delicate
cycle with like colors
(Wash alone the first time
to remove excess dye.)

Use only non-chlorine
bleach, if needed
Add fabric softener to
last rinse cycle.
Do not allow garment
to sit in washer.

Tumble dry low on wrinkle
release cycle. Remove
promptly.

Touch up with cool iron,
if needed.

DO NOT IRON THE DECORATION.
DO NOT DRY CLEAN.

Name _____   Date _____

Exploring Careers: Fashion Designer

A. Answer the following questions about a career as a fashion designer.

1. What three skills or abilities make a fashion designer successful?

    _____

    _____

2. What education do most fashion designers have?

    _____

3. What are four different companies or people a fashion designer might work for?

    _____

    _____

4. What does a fashion designer do once the design sketches are finished?

    _____

    _____

    _____

5. Why is teamwork with other professionals important in fashion design?

    _____

    _____

    _____

B. Use the Internet to research other possible career choices in this field and complete the chart.

Career	
Responsibilities	
Education Required	
Average Salary	
Is this a career you might pursue?	
Why or why not?	
Career	
Responsibilities	
Education Required	
Average Salary	
Is this a career you might pursue?	
Why or why not?	

Name _____ Date _____

"Uniforms: Just Right or All Wrong?"

A. Write one or more numbers next to each boldfaced word to show how well you know it.

5 I use it in everyday conversation.
4 I heard it on TV or on the radio.
3 I heard or used it in school.
2 I read it in a book, magazine, or online.
1 I have not read, heard, or used this word.

☐ **personal** (adj) *one's own; private or individual*
I prefer to keep my *personal* opinions to myself.

☐ **control** (v) *be in charge of; direct*
Sometimes it is hard for me to *control* my feelings.

☐ **conservative** (adj) *traditional or modest*
That long-sleeved blouse and plain black pants are very *conservative*.

☐ **focus** (v) *fix attention on something*
I tried to *focus* on my math homework, but her bright pink hair was too distracting.

☐ **individual** (n) *a single being or thing*
It takes a self-confident *individual* to wear that crazy-looking jacket.

B. Complete each sentence with the correct vocabulary word from Part A.

1. "Pay attention," our teacher said. "You must _____ on what you are doing."

2. Does the fashion industry _____ what you wear?

3. The color red does not look attractive on every _____ who wears it.

4. A T-shirt and jeans is my _____ fashion preference.

5. The new marching band uniforms have the usual _____ style.

Name _____ Date _____

Word Building

A. Build new words that have *person* as the base word. Add one or more word parts to the chart to build the words. Be sure the new word makes sense.

Prefix	*im-*				
Suffix	*-ify*	*-ity*	*-ize*	*-al*	*-ly*

Build New Words	Definitions
person	*human being*
1. personal	
2. personality	
3.	*make personal*
4. personally	*as far as oneself is concerned*
5. personify	
6.	*not showing or involving personal feelings*

B. Think about the meanings of the words in Part A and how you have heard each word used. Choose the word from Part A that BEST completes each sentence.

1. The students put labels with their names inside their uniforms to _____ them.

2. The keepsakes in that box are my _____ property.

3. Even if my brother wears a uniform, he doesn't act like a conservative _____.

4. Anna chooses clothes that express her friendly _____.

5. _____, I have strong opinions about uniforms.

6. The new school building had an _____ atmosphere because it had no pictures, statues, or trophy cases yet.

7. The proud sailors liked to _____ their ship by calling it "a great lady."

Name _____   Date _____

Author's Purpose/Bias

A. Reread "Uniforms: Just Right or All Wrong?" and find examples in each of the letters to the editor of the following types of bias.

Type of Bias	Chrissy Reynolds	Roberto Alvarez
1. exaggeration		
2. generalization		
3. loaded words		
4. opinions that appear as facts		

B. Think about whether you would be for or against school uniforms. Write statements defending your position using each of the techniques listed below.

1. exaggeration _____

   _____

2. generalization _____

   _____

3. loaded words _____

   _____

4. opinions that appear as facts _____

   _____

Name _____ Date _____

Write in Response to Reading

A. Could the same news story seem different when written by three different sources? Read the following news story summary. Then, read the three school newspaper headlines that tell about the same news story. For each headline, tell who you think wrote it and why. Underline any clues in the headline that helped you decide.

News Story Summary: Next year, all schools in the district will add 20 days to the school calendar. The school year will start two weeks earlier and end two weeks later than last year.

Summer Cut Short by Administrators

_____

_____

_____

Administration Finds Innovative Way to Improve Test Scores

_____

_____

_____

Will More Work Mean More Pay?

_____

_____

_____

B. Write a news story summary about an issue in your school related to uniforms, profiling, or fashions. Then, write three headlines that show different points of view or bias about the topic. Make sure your readers can detect the bias in the headlines.

News Story Summary:

_____

_____

_____

Headlines:

_____

_____

_____

Name _____ Date _____

Vocabulary

"In the Public Eye"

A. Rate your knowledge of each boldfaced word.

3   I know what this word means, and I can use it in a sentence.
2   I have an idea of this word's meaning, but I need to know more.
1   I don't know what this word means.

☐ **goods** (n) *things that can be bought or sold; products*
The United States imports *goods* from around the world.

☐ **loyal** (adj) *faithful to someone or something*
We have been *loyal* customers, shopping at the corner store for five years.

☐ **bias** (v) *cause someone's way of thinking to change to be in favor of or against*
Don't try to *bias* me against him. Let me make up my own mind.

☐ **manufacture** (v) *make products in large amounts*
The company can *manufacture* millions of computer parts each year.

☐ **consumers** (n) *people who buy products or services; customers*
Without *consumers* to buy what they sell, stores would go out of business.

B. Read each statement. Circle true or false.

1. If you **manufacture** something, you take it apart.   true   false

2. If you **bias** me against the movie, I won't want to see it.   true   false

3. **Consumers** buy only food.   true   false

4. You can never count on a friend who is **loyal**.   true   false

5. A clothing store does not sell **goods**.   true   false

C. Write three sentences about fashion. Use one boldfaced word from Part A in each sentence.

1. _____

2. _____

3. _____

Name _____ Date _____

Big Picture Notes

Notes about _____	Questions

Summary

Name _____   Date _____

Word Building

A. Build new words that have *consume, loyal*, or *bias* as the base word. Add a word part to build new words and identify the part of speech. Be sure the new word makes sense.

Inflectional Ending	-ed	-ing				Prefix	un-	dis-
Suffix	-able	-ly	-er	-al	-ty			

Build New Words with *-ing*, *-able*, and *-er*	Definitions
consume (v)	*buy or use*
1.	
2.	
3.	
with *-ly*, *-ty* and *dis-*	
loyal (adj)	*faithful*
4.	
5.	
6.	
with *-ed* and *un-*	
bias (v)	*prejudice someone; cause to have a one-sided view*
7. bias (n)	
8.	

B. Complete the paragraph. Use words that have *consume, loyal*, or *bias* as the base word.

Most of the time, I don't do much shopping. You wouldn't call me a big _____.

However, I am very _____ to one business. It's Bernie's Ice-Cream Shop. Bernie

has the best ice cream in the city. I'm not the only one at the shop _____ delicious

treats. Hundreds of people _____ ice cream there—more than at any other shop

I know. Bernie repays my _____ by giving me extra scoops. Of course, Bernie

happens to be my uncle. Would you believe that I have an _____ opinion?

Name _____ Date _____

Write in Response to Reading

A. Choose a real or imaginary product or service to sell. Create branding for the product or service. Record the name of the product or service in the chart and answer the questions.

Product or Service?	
How will it benefit people who use it?	
What group of people (age, gender, interests) is most likely to need it or use it?	
What group is least likely to need it or use it?	
What is the feeling you want the people who will use the product or service to have when they see this?	

B. To create branding for your product or service and company, design, write, and draw in the following spaces. Persuade people to buy your product or service and be loyal consumers to your brand.

Design a logo.	Write advertising copy.	Draw a product picture.

Name _____   Date _____

Review Vocabulary

A. Complete each sentence by writing a context clue that supports the meaning of the boldfaced word. A context clue can be an example, synonym, antonym, or brief explanation. The first one is done for you.

1. You can buy **goods**, such as ____**jeans and sweaters**____, at the mall.

2. Jared is **loyal**, or _____, to his favorite brand of running shoes.

3. Julie has a **bias** toward her favorite brand of jeans. She _____ _____ the way they look and fit.

4. Clothing companies **manufacture**, or _____, the clothes in large factories.

5. Crowds of **consumers**, or _____, came to the department store's sale.

B. Read the following dialogue. Write a word from the box that BEST completes each sentence. Use the words in parentheses as clues.

control	manufacture	individual	contradictory	focus
loyal	conservative	consumers	personal	bias

Joel: I can't stand the new school uniforms! They have totally taken away everybody's _____ (one's own; individual) style. My friends and I used to identify with our group by wearing the same styles and brand names. Now we can't.

Lina: So, you're upset at how the school tries to _____ (make) us to conform to a certain style. But, you and your friends already conform to one another so you fit in with the crowd. You are saying _____ (opposite) things.

Joel: Well, at least every _____ (a single person) made his or her own decision about what to wear. Now we have to wear these really _____ (traditional or modest) uniforms. We look like clones.

Lina: Before we had uniforms, some students felt like they couldn't fit in with the others. Maybe now students will _____ (fix attention on something) on learning rather than what message our clothes are sending about us.

Name _____   Date _____

Extend Vocabulary

A. The word *manufacture* uses the Latin roots *manus* and *factus*. The root *manus* means "hand." The root *factus* means "to make." Read the following words and their definitions. Notice how the meanings of the English words still contain the meanings of the Latin roots.

Words	Definitions
manually	*done by hand*
manuscript	*a document written by hand*
manicure	*a treatment for the hands; trimming and cleaning nails*

Words	Definitions
factory	*a building where products are assembled*
artifacts	*practical objects made by a person*
factors	*circumstances or facts that make or influence a result*

B. Complete each sentence with one of the words from Part A.

1. The clothing was sewn in a large _____ with many workers.

2. Jantira gave herself a _____ after one of her fingernails broke.

3. We admired the exhibit of vases and other _____ from Ancient Greece.

4. Long hours, dangerous work conditions, and low pay are _____ that make sweatshops cruel and unfair.

5. Nadia had to sew the buttons on her coat _____ with a needle and thread.

6. Shakespeare used a quill pen dipped in ink to write the _____ of his play.

C. Choose two words from Part A. Use a word with the root *manus* to write one sentence. Use a word with the root *factus* to write the second sentence.

1. _____

   _____

2. _____

   _____

Name _____ Date _____

Assess Comprehension and Vocabulary

A. Read the advertisements. Notice the bias and persuasive techniques in the text. Notice the difference between facts and opinions. Remember that bias is a strong preference for a point of view.

Advertisement 1

You have a personal sense of humor—so do our popular screen-printed T's. Express yourself. It's the fashion statement you'll want to make!

Advertisement 2

The greatest of the world's intellectuals wore tweed jackets. Our tweed is woven in Scotland. Look smart! Feel smart! Be a stylish individual! Wear our collection of tweed skirts, pants, and jackets.

Advertisement 3

The tie—at the center of your outfit. It commands attention. It inspires others to focus on you. It's the accessory that's worth spending money on for the best quality. Command attention. Get the respect you deserve only with our fine silk ties. None other can compete with our fabrics, patterns, and colors.

Advertisement 4

Control your game performance! Run faster and jump higher. Dwyane Wade is loyal to our basketball shoes. Nobody else knows better how to choose the right brand.

B. Circle the letter of each correct answer.

1. What is a synonym for the word *personal*?
   A. valuable
   B. ridiculous
   C. public
   D. own

2. What is an antonym for the word *individual*?
   A. person
   B. single
   C. group
   D. independent

3. Which word does NOT go with *focus*?
   A. ignore
   B. concentrate
   C. attention
   D. look

4. What goes with the word *control*?
   A. in focus
   B. in charge
   C. in favor
   D. in style

Name _____   Date _____

5. What is a synonym for the word *loyal*?
   A. false
   B. valued
   C. faithful
   D. friendly

6. Which persuasive technique is in Advertisement 1? Choose all that apply.
   A. exaggeration
   B. generalization
   C. loaded words
   D. none

7. Which persuasive technique is in Advertisement 2? Choose all that apply.
   A. exaggeration
   B. generalization
   C. loaded words
   D. none

8. Which persuasive technique is in Advertisement 3? Choose all that apply.
   A. exaggeration
   B. generalization
   C. loaded words
   D. none

9. Which persuasive technique is in Advertisement 4? Choose all that apply.
   A. exaggeration
   B. generalization
   C. loaded words
   D. none

10. Advertisement 1: —*so do our popular screen-printed T's.* Is this a statement of fact or opinion?
    A. fact
    B. opinion

11. Advertisement 2: *Our tweed is woven in Scotland.* Is this sentence a statement of fact or opinion?
    A. fact
    B. opinion

12. Advertisement 3: *It's the accessory that's worth spending money on for the best quality.* Is this sentence a statement of fact or opinion?
    A. fact
    B. opinion

13. Advertisement 4: *Nobody else knows better how to choose the right brand.* Is this sentence a statement of fact or opinion?
    A. fact
    B. opinion

14. Which word below is a loaded word from the ads?
    A. deserve
    B. commands
    C. loyal
    D. all of the above

Name _____ Date _____

15. What do the advertisements promise you will have if you buy each product?

_____

_____

_____

_____

_____

_____

Name _____   Date _____

Reteach

Read the advertisements. Answer the questions after each. Notice the bias and persuasive techniques in the text. Remember to notice the difference between facts and opinions. Remember that bias is a strong preference for a point of view.

LeatherLand Fashions

You're never fully dressed without our stunning genuine leather belts.

You'll like the way you look!

---

1. A word is **loaded** when it carries a meaning that tries to persuade you. To find a loaded word, ask yourself if you might agree or disagree. Which word might you disagree with if you saw the belts? Circle the word.

2. An **opinion** is a statement that you can't prove by measuring or in some other factual way. Underline opinions.

3. What do you think this ad wants you to feel about the belts? _____
   _____
   _____

4. Circle loaded words in the school uniforms ad.

5. Underline opinions.

6. What does the ad promise you will have or feel?
   _____
   _____
   _____

Classic School Uniforms

Walk into school knowing you will succeed. Our attractive school uniforms are the perfect solution for the learning environment.
The conservative look stimulates focus and concentration.

Confidence looks great on you!

Name _____ Date _____

Dream Sweaters

Cashmere is everybody's favorite wool.

Feel luxurious in our elegant sweaters

of the finest and softest cashmere.

You deserve the best, don't you?

7. A **generalization** is a statement that is too broad to be true. Generalizations use words like *everybody*, *most people*, *always*, and *never*. To find a generalization, ask yourself whether there could be an exception to the statement. Which sentence is a generalization in the sweater ad?

_____

_____

8. Why is it false? _____

_____

9. Circle loaded words.

10. What does the ad promise you will have or feel?

_____

11. Which sentence is a generalization in the track gear ad? _____

_____

_____

12. Why is it false? _____

_____

_____

13. Circle loaded words.

14. What does the ad promise you will have or feel?

_____

Leader Track Gear

You'll always achieve the

best warm-up before the big

race with our track pants.

Prepare with flair! Join

the best athletes with the

winning style.

Chill Fighters

I've worn other wool socks, but none kept my feet toasty warm like these. Comfort matters most. Stay warm through the winter with these high-quality Scottish wool socks.

15. Circle loaded words.

16. Underline an opinion.

17. What does the ad promise you will have or feel?

_____

Name _____ **Date** _____

fashionwarehouse

"Where Fashion Comes to You!"

HIGH FASHION CLOTHES AT BARGAIN-BASEMENT PRICES

Biggest sale of the season • Prices slashed to unbelievable lows
Huge inventory for the best selection

Designer dresses—trendy and fashionable
All the latest styles—solids, prints, stripes—just off the runway!
100% silk, cotton, linen, or wool—as well as blends of the best
synthetic fabrics on the market
Regularly priced from $139.99 to $199.99
Already marked-down prices ranging from **$40 to $80—deduct 15%**
Already marked-down prices ranging from **$90 to $110—deduct 20%**
Past-season bargain dresses now selling for $20 or less

Samples of our spectacular savings:

Fine imported wool
coats and jackets
*Retail priced
at $99.99*
**Now 25%
off our sale
price of $50**

Men's dress and casual slacks
Designer labels, high-quality
natural fabrics
Retail priced at $89.99
All under $40

Huge selection of updated shoes from a well-known Italian designer
Fine-grain leather and unusual synthetics
Full range of sizes and colors
A steal at $49 per pair, or two pairs for $80

Ethnic specialties—designs from all around the globe
Mexican embroidered blouses and shirts **just $15**
African caftans and robes **just $19.99**

Name _____   **Date** _____

1. Place a plus sign above strong, descriptive adjectives.

2. Highlight prices and discount percentages.

3. The words *trendy* and *fashionable* are examples of _____.

4. How much do past-season bargain dresses cost? _____

5. What percentage can you deduct for a $100 garment? _____

6. What kind of coats and jackets are on sale? _____

Name _____ **Date** _____

Exploring Careers: Retail Salesperson

A. Answer the following questions about a career as a retail salesperson.

1. What characteristics or abilities fit with a career as a retail salesperson?

   _____

   _____

2. Why are employees for the retail market always in high demand?

   _____

   _____

3. How do salespeople gain experience and learn skills?

   _____

   _____

4. What responsibilities do retail salespeople have?

   _____

   _____

   _____

5. How would a good memory be helpful for a position in retail sales?

   _____

   _____

B. Use the Internet to research other possible career choices in this field and complete the chart.

Career	
Responsibilities	
Education Required	
Average Salary	
Is this a career you might pursue?	
Why or why not?	
Career	
Responsibilities	
Education Required	
Average Salary	
Is this a career you might pursue?	
Why or why not?	

Name _____   Date _____

A. Organize Your Ideas

Animals: Heroes
and Scholars

-
-
-

How does animal
intelligence differ from
human intelligence?

-
-
-

What jobs can animals
perform better than
humans?

-
-
-

How do animals learn?

-
-
-

What else would you like to know about animal intelligence and bravery?

_____

_____

B. The Big Picture

Write the big idea of each passage in the outside ovals. Connect the passages in the center oval by
writing the big picture.

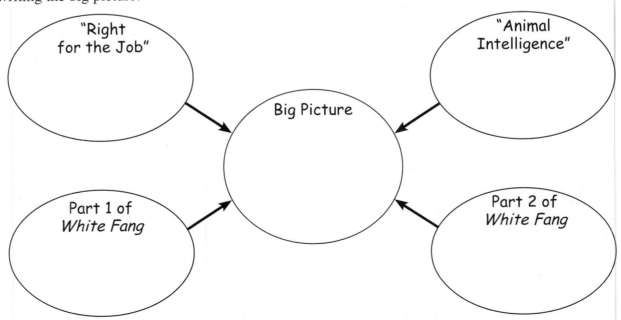

"Right
for the Job"

"Animal
Intelligence"

Big Picture

Part 1 of
White Fang

Part 2 of
White Fang

C. Expedition Dictionary

You will read the following vocabulary words throughout the Expedition. As you learn the words, use them as often as possible in your oral and written language.

"Right for the Job"

officials	(n) *people who hold important positions in an organization*
evaluate	(v) *decide the condition or value of someone or something after thinking carefully about it*
domestic	(adj) *to do with the home; not wild*
acute	(adj) *sharp*
discern	(v) *recognize or identify*
inquiry	(n) *examination of the facts; investigation*

"Animal Intelligence"

instinct	(n) *behavior that is natural, not learned*
complex	(adj) *very complicated; not simple*
conditioned	(adj) *learned*
stimulus	(n) *anything that causes an action*
associate	(v) *connect together*
exhibited	(v) *showed*

from *White Fang*, Part 1

characterized	(v) *marked or identified with certain qualities*
incorrigible	(adj) *difficult or impossible to control*
persecuted	(v) *treated someone cruelly and unfairly because of his or her ideas or beliefs*
vainly	(adv) *unsuccessfully; futilely*
compelled	(v) *made someone do something by giving him or her orders or using force*
infinitely	(adv) *endlessly; in a never-ending fashion*

from *White Fang*, Part 2

fiends	(n) *evil or cruel people*
commotion	(n) *a lot of noisy, excited activity*
abyss	(n) *a very deep hole that seems to have no bottom*
perceptibly	(adv) *clearly or noticeably*
tenacity	(n) *the quality of holding on firmly to something*
venture	(v) *put oneself at risk by doing something daring or dangerous*

Dictionary Challenge

Write five days of journal entries from one of the scientists studying animals using as many vocabulary words as possible.

Name _____ Date _____

Vocabulary

"Right for the Job"

A. Write one or more numbers next to each boldfaced word to show when you have seen, heard, or used this word.

5   I use it in everyday conversation.
4   I heard it on TV or on the radio.
3   I heard or used it in school.
2   I read it in a book, magazine, or online.
1   I have not read, heard, or used this word.

___ **officials** (n) *people who hold important positions in an organization*
The airport *officials* control what you can bring into the country.

___ **evaluate** (v) *decide the condition or value of someone or something after thinking carefully about it*
Dog trainers *evaluate* the skill level of a dog before deciding if it is ready to work.

___ **domestic** (adj) *to do with the home; not wild*
Domestic dogs are easier to train than wild dogs.

___ **acute** (adj) *sharp*
Dogs use their *acute* sense of smell to sniff out drugs and chemicals that humans can't smell.

___ **discern** (v) *recognize or identify*
Dogs can *discern* the voice of a man they have heard before.

___ **inquiry** (n) *examination of the facts; investigation*
The man's testimony led detectives to hold a murder *inquiry*.

B. Read each sentence, then answer the question.

1. If Liza has **acute** eyesight, does she need eyeglasses? _____

2. If Jorge can **discern** which dog is a sheepdog, can he identify it or tell how healthy it is?
   _____

3. If you were part of an **inquiry** to find a missing dog, would you try to nourish it or find information about it? _____

4. Would you find a **domestic** animal in a jungle or in a house? _____

5. Would you **evaluate** a zoo by how much you enjoyed it or by applying for a zoo job?
   _____

6. Do **officials** of a school take charge of it or attend classes there? _____

Name _____ Date _____

Word Building

A. By knowing one word, you often can have information about many words. Read the chart to learn new words that are related to some of your vocabulary words.

Words	Definitions
inquiry (n)	*examination of the facts; investigation*
inquire (v)	*ask*
inquisition (n)	*intense questioning; investigation*
inquisitive (adj)	*curious; always questioning*
evaluate (v)	*decide the condition or value of someone or something after thinking carefully about it*
evaluation (n)	*the process of rating something*
evaluator (n)	*a person who rates something*
officials (n)	*people who hold important positions in an organization*
official (adj)	*approved by someone in authority*

B. Complete each sentence with one of the words from Part A.

1. To get my driver's license, I had to read the _____ driving handbook.

2. Carmen was nervous as she waited for the judge's _____ of her project.

3. I was told to _____ about the rules of the tournament at the front desk.

4. It felt like an _____ when my mother asked me about coming in late.

5. The _____ for our club's budget checked our spending.

6. Carlos was very _____. He asked his mother questions all the time.

C. Choose three words from Part A. Write a sentence for each word.

1. _____

2. _____

3. _____

Name _____ Date _____

Main Idea and Details

A. Complete the diagram using information from "Right for the Job."

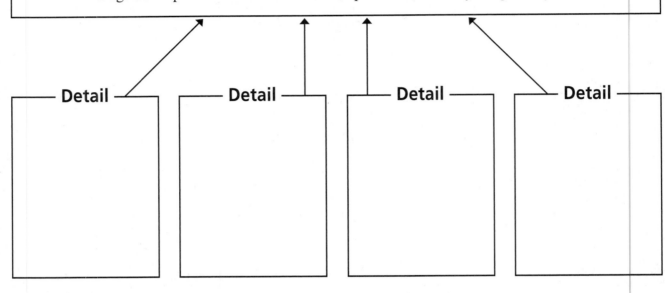

Main Idea

Dogs have special characteristics that help humans do many dangerous jobs.

Detail

Detail

Detail

Detail

B. Use the main idea and supporting details to write a brief summary of "Right for the Job."

_____

_____

_____

_____

_____

_____

_____

_____

_____

_____

_____

_____

_____

_____

_____

_____

Name _____   **Date** _____

Write in Response to Reading

Imagine these scenes at the beginning of "Right for the Job." Choose one scene and create a story with a beginning, middle, and end. You may tell your story from the animal or the owner's viewpoint.

• Roger slips into enemy territory to find the stranded troops.
• Missy and Clark determine whether airline travelers are carrying drugs.
• Sam helps Ms. Gomez cross the street.

_____
_____
_____
_____
_____
_____
_____
_____
_____
_____
_____
_____
_____
_____
_____
_____
_____
_____
_____
_____
_____
_____
_____
_____
_____

Name _____   Date _____

Vocabulary

"Animal Intelligence"

A. Put a check mark in each row to indicate how well you know each boldfaced word.

	Know This Word	Have Seen This Word	Don't Know This Word
instinct (n) *behavior that is natural, not learned* Lions don't need to be taught to hunt because it is an *instinct*.			
complex (adj) *very complicated; not simple* Some animals are intelligent enough to be taught to perform *complex* tasks.			
conditioned (adj) *learned* The *conditioned* behavior to repeat words is taught to parrots.			
stimulus (n) *anything that causes an action* The *stimulus* that causes dogs to salivate is the sound of the dinner bell.			
associate (v) *connect together* Dolphins *associate* signs with actions.			
exhibited (v) *showed* The monkeys *exhibited* very human-like behavior as we watched them.			

B. Choose the correct boldfaced word from Part A to answer each question.

1. Which word is related to an animal that has careful training or teaching? _____

2. Which word would you use to describe why dogs bark at strangers? _____

3. Which word describes a trick that requires doing four actions at once? _____

4. Which word describes how the word *leash* makes you think of *dog*? _____

5. Which word is the opposite of *hid* or *concealed*? _____

6. Think about working with dogs. Which word describes *whistle, treat*, and *command*?

    _____

Name _____ Date _____

Big Picture Notes

Notes about _____	Questions

Summary

Name _____ Date _____

Word Building

A. Some suffixes can change the meaning of a word. The suffix *-ion* can change some verbs into nouns. Read the words and their meanings. Notice some spelling changes in the verbs when they are changed to nouns.

Verbs
associate: *connect*
stimulate: *encourage*
graduate: *finish a course of study*
exhibit: *display or demonstrate*

+ *-ion*

Nouns
association: *a connected group*
stimulation: *an encouragement*
graduation: *the act of finishing*
exhibition: *a display or demonstration*

B. Choose a verb or noun from Part A to complete each sentence.

1. The students visited the zoo to see an _____ of primates.

2. You may _____ an aquarium with the ocean.

3. The friends plan to study marine biology after they _____ from high school.

4. Cats are often given yarn as a _____ to play.

5. People who take action to protect animals often belong to an _____.

6. Many animals _____ behaviors that humans find amazing.

C. Choose verbs and the corresponding nouns from Part A. Write sentences using both words.

Verb _____ Noun _____

Sentence _____

_____

Verb _____ Noun _____

Sentence _____

_____

Verb _____ Noun _____

Sentence _____

_____

Name _____ Date _____

Write in Response to Reading

Imagine there is research that conclusively proves animals are as intelligent as humans. How would your treatment or feeling about animals change as a result of this new knowledge? How would the world change?

If I knew that animals are truly as intelligent as humans, I would _____

_____

_____

_____

_____

_____

If animals were really as intelligent as humans, life around the world would _____

_____

_____

_____

_____

_____

_____

_____

_____

_____

_____

_____

_____

_____

_____

_____

_____

_____

_____

_____

Name _____   Date _____

Review Vocabulary

A. Read the paragraph. Replace each underlined word or phrase with a vocabulary word that is its antonym.

> My family and I went to a dolphin performance. The dolphins live in an aquarium and are trained like 1. <u>wild</u> animals. Dolphins have well-developed, 2. <u>weak</u> senses of sight and hearing. They use these senses for communication. The dolphins we saw 3. <u>concealed</u> their ability to obey the trainers' hand signals. Dolphins also produced 4. <u>simple</u> whistle sounds to communicate with one another. They had unique whistles that they 5. <u>don't connect</u> with individual dolphins. It's as if they know one another's names. To learn more about dolphin communication, researchers pose many questions, then they conduct an 6. <u>conclusion</u>. We aren't scientists, but if you ask us, dolphins can talk.

1. _____   4. _____

2. _____   5. _____

3. _____   6. _____

B. Complete each sentence by writing a context clue that supports the meaning of the boldfaced word. The first one is done for you.

1. Birds know how to build nests by **instinct**, which is <u>**a behavior that is natural and not learned**</u>.

2. The pigeons developed a **conditioned** behavior to get food. The behavior was not _____
_____.

3. In autumn, a **stimulus**, such as _____, causes birds to fly south.

4. In the subway, **officials**, such as _____, use trained dogs that can detect the scent of illegal drugs.

5. A dog trainer needs to **evaluate** a dog's skills before it can work for a police department. The trainer _____
_____.

6. Dolphins are able to **discern**, or _____, the exact location of an object by making clicking sounds.

Name _____   Date _____

Extend Vocabulary

A. The word *associate* uses the Latin root *socius*, meaning "sharing, group, people." Read the words and their meanings. Notice how all the word meanings connect to the words *sharing, group,* and *together.*

associate	*connect together*
socialize	*visit; interact with others*
association	*organization; a connected group that shares a purpose*
social	*liking to live with others or in a community*
society	*community with shared customs and laws*

B. Think about the meanings of the words in Part A and how you have heard each word used. Choose the word that BEST completes each sentence.

1. Dogs enjoy playing with their owners. They are _____ creatures.

2. Pavlov taught dogs to _____ food with the sound of a bell.

3. The dolphins _____ by swimming together and whistling to one another.

4. Trained dogs have very important jobs in our _____.

5. You can join an _____ that rescues lost and wounded pets.

C. Read the following verb forms, then complete each sentence with the correct verb.

associate	**associated**	**associating**	**socialize**	**socialized**	**socializing**

1. After I saw lions in the zoo, I _____ them with courage and power.

2. When dolphins communicate, they are _____ with one another.

3. The two dogs at the park _____ with each other by barking and sniffing.

4. The children were laughing and waving at the zoo animals. They were _____ the wild animals with their stuffed toys or with characters in cartoons.

Name _____   Date _____

Assess Comprehension and Vocabulary

A. Read the passage. Notice important details and main ideas that are stated indirectly in the text.

Special Dogs for Special Jobs

Dogs have helped humans for centuries. Their size, strength, and acute senses of hearing, smell, and sight make them perfect partners for certain tasks. Not all dogs are alike though. Certain breeds are favored for specific conditioned tasks.

Detection Dogs

What do detection dogs search for? Bombs, land mines, and illegal drugs are a few of the things they look for. These dogs use their strong sense of smell to discern particular odors. Airport security officials often use the help of detection dogs to screen luggage. The most common breeds for this task are Labrador or Chesapeake Bay retrievers, German shepherds, Belgian Malinois, and beagles. They are quick learners and persistent searchers.

Search-and-Rescue Dogs

Search-and-rescue dogs need physical capabilities to fit in tight and rugged spaces like building rubble and the wilderness. They need to pick up the scents of missing people. German shepherds, Labrador and golden retrievers, and Newfoundlands have exhibited the strength, courage, and persistence for this work. They go on missions that often take days or weeks to complete.

B. Circle the letter of each correct answer.

1. What is a synonym for the word *acute*?
   A. sharp
   B. inaccurate
   C. dull
   D. tiny

2. What is a synonym for the word *conditioned*?
   A. forced
   B. intelligent
   C. examined
   D. learned

3. What is NOT a synonym for the word *discern*?
   A. recognize
   B. identify
   C. obey
   D. detect

4. What is the BEST definition of the word *officials*?
   A. people who hold important positions
   B. the condition or value of people or things
   C. the place where important people work
   D. examination of the facts; investigation

Name _____ Date _____

5. What would be another good title for the passage?
   A. A Career as a Dog Breeder
   B. Dog Breeds with Skills for Special Jobs
   C. How to Train Different Dog Breeds
   D. Different Dog Breeds: Pets and Workers

6. What is the general topic of this passage?
   A. dog breeds and training
   B. dog breeds and jobs
   C. dogs as quick learners
   D. dogs that are excellent rescuers

7. Which is NOT an important detail?
   A. They have exhibited strength, courage, and persistence.
   B. They need to fit in tight and rugged spaces.
   C. Dogs have been helping humans for centuries.
   D. They are quick learners and persistent searchers.

8. Which dog breed is NOT often a search-and-rescue dog?
   A. Newfoundland
   B. German shepherd
   C. golden retriever
   D. beagle

9. What trait is most important for detection dogs?
   A. courage
   B. acute sense of smell
   C. strength
   D. acute vision

10. What trait is NOT mentioned about search-and-rescue dogs?
    A. acute hearing
    B. fit in tight and rugged spaces
    C. persistence
    D. acute sense of smell

11. *Certain breeds are favored for specific conditioned tasks.*
    Who do you think favors certain breeds?
    A. people who operate a dog shelter
    B. people who are in an emergency
    C. people who train dogs for jobs
    D. people who are passengers on airplanes

12. What can you infer is the reason that search-and-rescue dogs go on such long missions?
    A. The disaster usually occurs far from their training camp.
    B. Labradors lack the necessary skills for the job.
    C. It takes a long time to clean up disaster areas.
    D. The dogs are not quick.

13. What is the main idea of this passage?
    A. Detection dogs need to be quick learners and persistent searchers.
    B. Detection and search-and-rescue dogs save people's lives.
    C. Certain dog breeds have traits that make them better for certain jobs.
    D. Search-and-rescue dogs need to pick up scents of missing people.

Name _____ Date _____

14. Which of the following has allowed dogs to help humans for centuries?
    A. acute sense of hearing, smell, and sight
    B. size
    C. strength
    D. all of the above

15. Use the important details and the main idea to write a brief passage summary. Your summary should be at least three sentences.

    _____
    _____
    _____
    _____
    _____
    _____
    _____
    _____
    _____

Name _____   Date _____

Reteach

A. Read the passage. Look for the main idea as you read.

> Denyse is a lovable chimpanzee. When she was a newborn, a couple purchased her from a zoo and raised her like a human in their household. She grew up like a daughter to them. Denyse ate human food like fruit, marshmallows, pie filling, and pizza. After many years, one of her owners died. Then the other became too old to care for her. Denyse was sent to a center for chimpanzees. The center is in the middle of a tropical forest that closely resembles chimpanzees' native habitat. At the center, she has had to adjust to a new diet of fresh leaves, fruits, and vegetables. These are foods she would have naturally eaten in the wild. Denyse also has had to get used to socializing with other chimps. Because she was used to only being around people, she didn't like other chimps at first. Denyse is adapting to life with other chimps in her native home. It's a great challenge.

B. Answer the following questions.

1. What is the topic of the passage?

   _____

2. The main idea is indirectly stated in the passage. State the main idea.

   _____

   _____

3. Skim the passage. What are five important details in the passage?

   _____

   _____

   _____

   _____

   _____

4. What is one less important detail?

   _____

Name _____ Date _____

C. A main idea statement should state the main idea clearly. Write your original main idea from Part B, then expand, or add to, the main idea. Use information from the most important details to help you expand the statement.

Original Main Idea

_____

_____

_____

_____

Expanded Main Idea

_____

_____

_____

_____

D. Use the important details and the main idea to write a brief passage summary. Your summary should be at least three sentences.

_____

_____

_____

_____

_____

_____

Name _____   Date _____

A. As you read the newsletter, determine the main idea of each paragraph.

Elephant Slaves

Bamboo whips crackle in the air as a tremendous elephant strains to pull a huge log, weighing a ton or more, from a rain forest in Myanmar. This wild beast, forced into domestic service, trumpets loudly with the extreme effort. The sound fills me with despair. The elephant's trainer, called a mahout, is yelling at the elephant, ordering it to pull harder. He wants the elephant to haul the log down to the water. I want to see the elephant not chained up to haul a log, not being whipped, and not being yelled at by its trainer.

Suddenly, the heavy chain that links the elephant to the log snaps, and the elephant falls to the ground stunned. A wound on the elephant's stomach begins to bleed, yet the mahout is screaming at the elephant to get up and back to work. How could anyone treat such a majestic animal so cruelly? Using elephants for such dangerous and difficult work should be illegal.

An elephant belongs in the wild rain forests where it can associate with other elephants, raise its young in peace, and live out its 60-year life span in nature. Asian elephants once grazed along rivers in China. In fact, elephants used to graze over millions of square miles of Asia. Today, their habitat is about 95 percent smaller. Now, they are threatened by economic activity that makes them slaves to lumber producers.

This situation is especially important because the world's population of wild elephants may be decreasing at an alarming rate. Officials have no exact knowledge of the number of remaining Asian elephants, but the latest record suggests about 30,000. To force these elephants against their instinct to work in the forests seems a terrible waste of a beautiful creature. The work threatens their health and longevity and makes their lives a continual series of burdens for the benefit of whom? Is it for people who make money selling lumber? What is money compared with preserving the life of elephants?

Every day in the logging camps, elephants are chained to burdensome logs that they have learned to pull precariously downhill into nearby rivers. Their training for the job begins with permanent leg chains. Mahouts also prod the animals with sharp sticks to teach them what to do, and they jerk the elephants' trunks upward with rope to train them to release what they pick up. Elephants

begin working at about 20 years old and work for 35 years until their life is almost over and they are retired.

The difficult work of hauling timber causes injury to the working elephants. The spines of the elephants suffer incredible stress, and the usually supple skin becomes marked with lesions and scars. Moreover, we cannot tell how much the elephants suffer from being ripped from their family groups and moved into logging camps.

Most of you have probably seen elephants in a zoo. To see these intelligent and regal creatures in the wild as I have, then to see them struggling in chains, makes the message very clear to me. Help the official "Save the Elephants" campaign as it fights to stop elephants from logging. Write to us and give us your support. Then, visit India and see the animal you have helped rescue from slavery.

Name _____ Date _____

B. Write the unstated main idea of each paragraph.

Paragraph 1:

Paragraph 2:

Paragraph 3:

Paragraph 4:

Paragraph 5:

Paragraph 6:

Paragraph 7:

C. Use the main ideas you wrote in Part B to summarize the article in three sentences.

_____

_____

_____

_____

D. This is an example of a newsletter. Newsletters often are written to provide information for a particular group. Answer the following questions about the newsletter.

1. What is the author's point of view about elephants working in logging camps?

_____

2. Does the newsletter exhibit bias? Give examples from the text to support your response.

_____

_____

3. What actions do you think the author would like for people to take after reading the newsletter?

_____

_____

_____

Name _____ Date _____

Exploring Careers: Animal Trainer

A. Answer the following questions about a career as an animal trainer.

1. What are three different things an animal trainer might train an animal to do?

   _____

   _____

2. What education do most animal trainers have?

   _____

3. What is the range of salaries for animal trainers in the United States?

   _____

4. What are some ways to gain experience to become an animal trainer?

   _____

   _____

5. How could a career as an animal trainer be rewarding?

   _____

   _____

   _____

B. Use the Internet to research other possible career choices in this field and complete the chart.

Career	
Responsibilities	
Education Required	
Average Salary	
Is this a career you might pursue?	
Why or why not?	
Career	
Responsibilities	
Education Required	
Average Salary	
Is this a career you might pursue?	
Why or why not?	

Name _____ Date _____

Vocabulary

from *White Fang*, Part 1

A. Rate your knowledge of each boldfaced word.

   3   I know what this word means, and I can use it in a sentence.

   2   I have an idea of this word's meaning, but I need to know more.

   1   I don't know what this word means.

☐ **characterized** (v) *marked or identified with certain qualities*
The man is *characterized* as ferocious and uncontrollable because he always starts fights.

☐ **incorrigible** (adj) *difficult or impossible to control*
When he wasn't treated fairly, the *incorrigible* man began to destroy things.

☐ **persecuted** (v) *treated someone cruelly and unfairly because of his or her ideas or beliefs*
The prisoner thought he was *persecuted* when he had to spend days in solitary confinement.

☐ **vainly** (adv) *unsuccessfully; futilely*
I *vainly* searched for the uncatchable prisoner.

☐ **compelled** (v) *made someone do something by giving him or her orders or using force*
He wanted to run, but the guard *compelled* him to stay.

☐ **infinitely** (adv) *endlessly; in a never-ending fashion*
He was *infinitely* punished for the crimes of his youth.

B. Read each statement. Circle true or false.

1. If you put a leash on your dog and began walking, you **compelled** it to come with you.   true   false

2. If you searched for and found a lost cat, you searched **vainly**.   true   false

3. If a person is **characterized** as polite, he never greets you.   true   false

4. People have been **persecuted** for their beliefs.   true   false

5. If you look at up at the night sky, the stars appear to go on **infinitely**.   true   false

6. An **incorrigible** child follows instructions well.   true   false

Name _____ Date _____

Word Building

A. Knowing root words can help us understand new words. The Latin roots *sequ, secu,* and *sue* mean "to follow." Read words that use these roots.

consequence (n)	*something that follows as a result of an event or action*
sequence (n)	*follows an order of things, actions, or events*
subsequently (adv)	*following something else in time or order*
consecutive (adj)	*following one after another without a break or interruption*
ensue (v)	*follow closely after something*
pursue (v)	*work at something or carry it out; follow a process to completion*

B. Complete each sentence with one of the boldfaced words from Part A.

1. Jim Hall could have been given the death penalty as a _____ of his actions.

2. After his attack on the guard, Hall was _____ sent to solitary confinement.

3. If a criminal escaped from prison, a search to find him would _____.

4. Judge Scott had to _____ the line of questioning that led to Hall's conviction.

5. Hall was sentenced to two _____ life terms in prison.

6. The warden could not believe the _____ of events that led to Jim Hall's escape.

C. Choose three words from Part A. Write a sentence for each word.

1. _____

2. _____

3. _____

Name _____   Date _____

Story Elements

A. Scan the Anthology pages 209–212, from *White Fang*, Part 1. Complete the following chart.

Problem	Solution
Jim Hall wants to kill Judge Scott.	

B. In Part 1 of *White Fang*, the characters face other problems or conflicts. Read each quotation that describes a problem. Write the problem in your own words, then tell how the conflict or problem is solved. Use the Anthology pages to find your answers.

1. "After this, Jim Hall went to live in the incorrigible cell. He lived there three years. . . . He hated all things."

Problem	Solution

2. "Judge Scott . . . did not know . . . that Jim Hall was guiltless of the crime charged. And Jim Hall . . . did not know that Judge Scott was merely ignorant."

Problem	Solution

3. "Now White Fang was not a house dog, nor was he permitted to sleep in the house."

Problem	Solution

Name _____   **Date** _____

Write in Response to Reading

Imagine that you are Jim Hall and have been in prison for a year for a crime you did not commit. Use details from the passage and your own ideas to create Jim's journal entry.

Day 365

I am going mad! Each day I _____

_____

_____

_____

_____

_____

_____

_____

_____

_____

_____

_____

_____

_____

_____

_____

_____

_____

_____

_____

_____

_____

_____

_____

_____

_____

_____

Name _____ Date _____

Vocabulary

from *White Fang*, Part 2

A. Rate your knowledge of each boldfaced word.

3   familiar
2   somewhat familiar
1   unknown word

☐ **fiends** (n) *evil or cruel people*
The *fiends* attacked the prison guards.

☐ **commotion** (n) *a lot of noisy, excited activity*
The *commotion* made during the fight awoke the whole house.

☐ **abyss** (n) *a very deep hole that seems to have no bottom*
The dog jumped through the *abyss* of night, hoping to land on the intruder.

☐ **perceptibly** (adv) *clearly or noticeably*
The girls noticed that White Fang was *perceptibly* stronger than before.

☐ **tenacity** (n) *the quality of holding on firmly to something*
The wolf's *tenacity* for life kept him living.

☐ **venture** (v) *put oneself at risk by doing something daring or dangerous*
After his surgery, the wolf found it difficult to *venture* out into the dangers of the world.

B. Complete each sentence with the correct vocabulary word from Part A.

1. The submarine blindly descended into the _____ of the ocean.

2. In a horror movie, _____ often will attack innocent people.

3. The fire alarm caused a big _____ as people tried to escape from the building.

4. The young puppies were _____ tired after walking one block.

5. Because you might get lost or attacked by an animal, you should not _____ into the woods at night.

6. He tried and failed several times to prove his innocence, but he had the _____ to keep presenting his case to the judge.

Name _____ Date _____

Word Building

A. Read the following definitions, then use synonyms and antonyms from the box to complete the chart.

brutes	detectably	disturbance	friends	invisibly
monsters	obviously	silence	uproar	visibly

Words	Definitions	Synonyms	Antonyms
commotion	*a lot of noisy, excited activity*		
fiends	*evil or cruel people*		
perceptibly	*clearly or noticeably*		

B. Replace each underlined antonym with the correct vocabulary word from the first column in Part A.

1. The great <u>silence</u> woke the Scott family in the middle of the night. _____

2. Criminals can become <u>friends</u> if they are treated like animals. _____

3. White Fang would <u>invisibly</u> move and twitch when he was dreaming. _____

C. Write your own sentences using the following synonym pairs. Include both synonyms in the same sentence. The first one is done for you.

1. **commotion** and **disturbance** **When White Fang attacked the prisoner, it caused a great commotion, or disturbance.**

2. **perceptibly** and **visibly** _____

3. **fiends** and **brutes** _____

Name _____   Date _____

Story Elements—Climax

Read the meanings of rising action, climax, and other plot elements. Complete the diagram.

Climax
The climax in White Fang is when

Rising Action
events and problems or conflict
that create suspense

Event 4

Falling Action
The conflict is resolved. In *White Fang*, the conflict is resolved because

Event 3

White Fang: Parts 1 and 2

Event 2

Event 1
Jim Hall is sentenced to prison.

Resolution
What is the resolution to the main problem of Jim Hall wanting revenge?

Name _____ Date _____

Write in Response to Reading

Imagine that Part 2 begins differently. Read this version of the event, then complete the new ending for Part 2.

Sierra Vista awoke with alarm. Judge Scott rushed to the stairs. White Fang lay still, and Hall was turning to run out the door. Suddenly Jim Hall froze. He heard Judge Scott's booming voice. "Hall, I know you were innocent!"

_____

_____

_____

_____

_____

_____

_____

_____

_____

_____

_____

_____

_____

_____

_____

_____

_____

_____

_____

_____

_____

_____

_____

_____

_____

_____

_____

_____

Name _____   Date _____

Review Vocabulary

A. Complete each sentence by writing a context clue that supports the meaning of the boldfaced word.

1. The space shuttle launched into the **abyss**, or _____, of space.

2. People who are cruel and evil are **fiends**, or _____.

3. The dog was **perceptibly**, or _____, starving because you could see its ribs.

4. Looking up, the mountain seemd to reach **infinitely**, or _____ toward the sky.

5. After the robbery, the burglar **vainly**, or _____, attempted to avoid the police.

6. The man was full of anger after many years of being **persecuted**, or _____.

B. Write a word from the box that BEST completes each sentence.

tenacity	venture	commotion	compelled	incorrigible	characterized

We are outside the prison. Joe Garmen is walking out, a free man after 20 years in jail. Many people are celebrating his release, and others hold signs saying they oppose it. In the middle of this _____ outside the prison, reporters interview Garmen.

Reporter 1: Did you ever give up hope that you would be released one day?

Joe Garmen: The lonely days _____ me to do a lot of thinking. Sometimes I doubted I could make it, but I had the _____ to keep fighting to prove my innocence.

Reporter 2: What work will you do to make a living?

Joe Garmen: I met many people in prison. Some of them are _____ people, and some want to become good members of society. I would like to work with groups who help convicts after they are released.

Reporter 1: So, Mr. Garmen, now that you can _____ out in the world again, what do you want to do?

Joe Garmen: Before my imprisonment, I wouldn't have _____ myself as adventurous. But now, I want to try skydiving or scuba diving.

Reporter 2: Good luck to you, Mr. Garmen. Enjoy your freedom!

Name _____   Date _____

Extend Vocabulary

A. Each of the following words has the Latin root *ceive, cept,* or *captu.* They have the meaning "to take" or "to catch." Read the words and their meanings.

receive (v)	*get or take something*
deceive (v)	*trick, take advantage of, or mislead somebody*
accept (v)	*take something offered; come to terms*
intercept (v)	*stop, catch, or interrupt before completion or arrival*
capture (v)	*hold or catch the attention of someone*

B. Choose the boldfaced word from Part A that BEST completes each sentence.

1. Jim Hall did not _____ a fair trial.

2. After Hall escaped, he was able to _____ everyone who looked for him.

3. Many people searched for Jim Hall, but they did not _____ him.

4. The Scotts were too late to _____ White Fang's attack.

5. If Judge Scott told Jim Hall he was sorry, do you think Hall would _____ the apology?

C. Use a dictionary to find the definitions of the following words.

1. reception _____

2. deception _____

3. interception _____

What do these words have in common?

_____

_____

Name _____   Date _____

Assess Comprehension and Vocabulary

A. Read the following passage. Think about story elements as you read.

Carlos Garza looked out his office window, sighed, and bit into his ham sandwich. Being in a new city without family or friends was difficult. As Carlos took another bite, he glanced up to see a skinny, stray dog chasing a fast-food bag. It ran directly into the path of a rumbling dump truck. The truck screeched and slid into the ditch, nicking the dog's hind leg. The dog crumpled to the ground and lay still. The driver got out of the cab, yelling and cursing. A mother walking nearby with her toddler stopped. She began scolding the driver for his foul language. The driver argued loudly. She thought he was incorrigible. The scene compelled an older man to stop and calm them both. The injured dog was forgotten in the commotion.

Carlos had put his sandwich in his pocket and rushed to the scene. He saw the dog limping toward an abandoned garage. It was perceptibly hurt. Carlos called, "Here, boy," but the dog went inside. He followed.

Carlos's eyes adjusted to the dark abyss of the garage. He could discern an old car, rusted through and missing its doors and wheels. He heard rustling and whimpering from inside the car. The dog was lying with its back toward Carlos. It growled and snapped, baring its teeth. Carlos remembered the half-eaten sandwich in his pocket. "Here, boy. Have a bite." He tossed a small piece toward the dog. It gulped the piece and began sniffing for more. Carlos moved closer, extending the sandwich as he softly talked to the dog to calm it. "Nice boy, nice boy." The dog shifted to snatch the last bit of ham from his fingers. Carlos gasped. Five wiggling bundles of fur snuggled into the dog's chest. Pups! The dog nudged Carlos gently. Carlos smiled. It looked like he was going to have friends here after all.

B. Circle the letter of each correct answer.

1. Which word does NOT go with *perceptibly*?

   A. clearly

   B. visibly

   C. invisibly

   D. noticeably

2. Why does the driver's behavior seem *incorrigible*?

   A. He cursed the wounded dog and argued with onlookers.

   B. He hit the dog with the truck and caused it to die.

   C. He told the woman to call the police.

   D. He took the dog to the veterinarian.

Name _____ Date _____

3. Which of these things is NOT associated with a *commotion*?
   A. loud voices
   B. noise
   C. silence
   D. excitement

4. What made the interior of the garage feel like an *abyss*?
   A. the garbage
   B. the light
   C. the dampness
   D. the darkness

5. What is an antonym for the word *compelled*?
   A. forced
   B. obligated
   C. invited
   D. required

6. What is the MAJOR problem in the story?
   A. The dog is injured and needs help.
   B. The driver and the woman are fighting.
   C. Carlos is lonely and has no friends.
   D. The driver doesn't care that he injured the dog.

7. What is the solution to the major problem in question 6?
   A. The dog disappears.
   B. The driver calls a tow truck.
   C. Carlos buys a new lunch.
   D. Carlos takes care of the dog.

8. What surprise is revealed at the end?
   A. The stray dog is a wolf.
   B. The stray dog is a new mother.
   C. The stray dog has killed a man.
   D. The stray dog escaped from a kennel.

9. Why do you think the dog was growling and snapping at Carlos?
   A. It was hungry.
   B. It was protecting the pups.
   C. It was happy.
   D. It wanted to find a new home.

10. Why was the dog able to sneak away from the scene of the accident?
    A. The driver and the woman didn't notice the dog.
    B. The truck scared the dog but did not injure it.
    C. The dog belonged to Carlos and was hiding from him.
    D. The people who cared about the dog went for help.

11. Problems and complications create drama in a story. When you recognize a problem, you also must think about the solution. Reread the following sentence. What is the problem? *Being in a new city without family or friends was difficult.*
    A. Carlos was lonely.
    B. The city was too large.
    C. No one liked Carlos.
    D. Carlos wanted privacy.

Name _____   Date _____

12. Reread the following sentences. How was the problem from question 11 resolved in the passage?

    The dog nudged Carlos gently. Carlos smiled. It looked like he was going to have friends here after all.

    A. The dog wanted Carlos to leave it alone.
    B. The dog and pups would have to go to the shelter.
    C. The dog would be safe with Carlos.
    D. The dog and pups would be Carlos's new friends.

13. Which event does NOT contribute to the drama and tension in the story?

    A. The dog gets hit by the truck.
    B. The driver and pedestrians argue.
    C. Carlos eats his sandwich.
    D. Carlos follows the dog into the garage.

14. Which of the following is NOT a part of the setting of the story?

    A. Carlos's house
    B. an abandoned garage
    C. a street
    D. an office

15. Which statement is NOT a problem and solution in the passage?

    A. The dog is injured, so it goes to the garage to recover.
    B. Carlos sees the accident, so he calls the police to help.
    C. The dog is hungry, so Carlos feeds it his sandwich.
    D. The dog doesn't trust Carlos, so he talks softly and feeds it.

Name _____   Date _____

Reteach

A. Read a different version of the attack involving White Fang and Jim Hall. Think about problems/ solutions, rising action, and climax.

An Unexpected Ending

For an eternity, the strange god deliberated at the foot of the stairs. Then, instead of ascending, he froze. White Fang growled deep in his throat and let out a warning bark. The man backed unseen into the shadows of the great hall. White Fang barked again. Warning! Stranger in the house!

Judge Scott appeared at the top of the stairs and bellowed for Alice.

"What is that mongrel doing in our home?" Judge Scott asked Alice. "Put him out where he belongs!"

Alice, bleary-eyed from being rousted from bed, nodded numbly and headed down the stairs. Judge Scott pointed a finger at White Fang and yelled, "Quiet!", before stomping to his room and slamming the door.

Alice descended the steps. White Fang barked wildly. He started up the steps toward Alice, growling and baring his teeth. White Fang had to keep her away from the insane intruder waiting to harm her! Alice's eyes grew wide. She backed up the stairs and ran down the hall to get Weedon's help. In a flash, Weedon appeared at the top of the stairs with his gun.

White Fang barked rabidly, foam flecking and spraying as his agitation increased. The man was right behind the door! Could they not see him? Could they not smell him? As White Fang approached the stairs, Weedon held the shotgun to his shoulder, took aim, and fired.

The man dropped to the floor with a sickening thud.

B. Read the possible solutions for the problems. Circle each correct solution for the problem in the box.

Problem	Solution
The intruder is going to harm the Scotts.	1. Weedon fires at the intruder. 2. Weedon fires at White Fang.

Problem	Solution
Jim Hall is hiding in the house.	1. White Fang scratches at the door. 2. White Fang barks to warn the family.

Name _____ Date _____

Problem	Solution
Jim Hall will attack Alice if she comes downstairs.	1. White Fang growls at Alice to keep her upstairs.
	2. Judge Scott tells Alice to put White Fang out.

C. Read these events. They are the rising action that leads to the climax. Complete the graphic organizer by putting the events in the order they happened. Then, write the climax of the story.

White Fang tries to stop Alice from coming down by barking and growling.
Weedon appears with a shotgun in hand.
White Fang sees Hall and barks a warning.
Judge Scott tells Alice to put White Fang out.

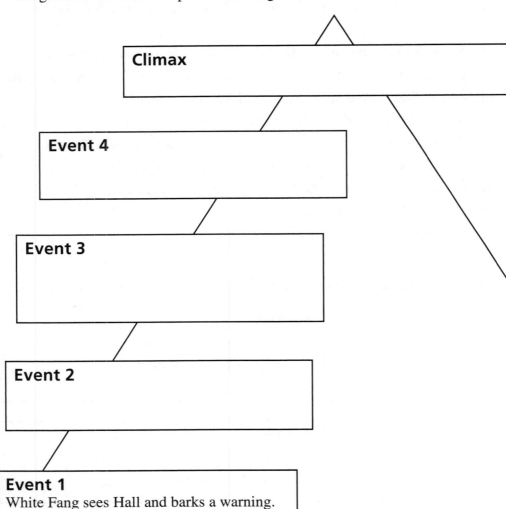

Climax

Event 4

Event 3

Event 2

Event 1
White Fang sees Hall and barks a warning.

Name _____   Date _____

Real World—Pet Adoption Notices

A. Read the following adoption notices.

Find-A-Pet Adoption Agency—The Cat's Meow

Our agency has 100 kittens and cats waiting to be adopted by cat-loving families. Drop in at our main shelter Monday–Saturday from noon–3:00 p.m. or Sunday from 11:00 a.m.– 5 p.m. Or, call for an appointment any day of the week, and one of our devoted animal service workers will assist you in finding the right pet or pets for your home.

Here are descriptions of our newcomers in case one is just the right cat for you.

Cirrus is a 2-year-old domestic short hair, white with black-tipped ears and tail. Cirrus is an extremely lovable cat that seems compelled to purr as soon as you reach out to pat her head. Cirrus needs a quiet pet-free home because her previous owner had a dog that persecuted her by chasing her away from her food.

Ro-meow is a 7-month-old, part Siamese, part Burmese mix. Ro-meow is very friendly and talkative, but he would prefer to be the only cat in the household. He hides whenever there is a commotion at the pet shelter, as if he were being pursued by fiends. But, when you are alone with Ro-meow, you can tell he's a very affectionate cat.

Lucy and Laura are two 5-month-old Russian blue kittens, pure gray. We think Lucy and Laura would love to stay together since they are inseparable playmates and hardly venture more than a few feet from each other in the outdoor yard at the shelter. If you have room for these two sweeties, they'll provide you with a lot of entertainment and fun. Can you imagine them cuddled up together on your sofa? What could be cuter than that?

Jester is a 3-year-old domestic short-hair orange tabby. Jester is an incorrigible "pouncer" who leaps at anyone who passes by him. Unless you want to play with Jester all day long, he might benefit from a home with a lively puppy or a kitten. Jester came to the shelter just a week ago, and everyone here absolutely loves this lively fellow.

Sherlock is a 6-year-old pure black long hair. Sherlock is a beautiful mature cat. His owners were compelled to move and could not take him, so they are hoping that Sherlock will find a caring home. At the shelter, Sherlock is quite shy, and he often stays by himself in a corner of the yard. He watches everything going on and seems to perceive all the actions and reactions of the other cats. If you're willing to spend a little time to help him adjust to your home, you will find Sherlock to be a fascinating pet.

Name _____   Date _____

Melody is a 6-month-old tortoise shell with blue eyes. Melody is the latest addition to our shelter. She is a cat that craves attention. With the tenacity of a bulldog but not the toughness, Melody will follow you around, mewing sweetly. All you have to do is put your hand in front of her, and she'll push her head gently against it as she purrs her appreciation loudly. Melody loves to be brushed, and her former owners tell us she is very good with children. We think Melody would be fine on her own in a loving household or with another gentle-natured cat or dog.

B. Answer each question.

1. What is the name of the shelter?

   _____

2. What are the days and hours of operation?

   _____

   _____

3. How many cats and kittens are available for adoption right now?

   _____

4. What is the benefit of adopting a cat from a shelter?

   _____

   _____

   _____

   _____

5. Would you adopt a pet? If so, how would you choose your pet? If not, why?

   _____

   _____

   _____

   _____

   _____

6. Write your own ad for a stray cat. Don't forget to include what the cat looks like, its name, and its best qualities.

   _____

   _____

   _____

   _____

   _____

   _____

   _____

Name _____ Date _____

Exploring Careers: Veterinarian

A. Answer the following questions about a career as a veterinarian, animal technician, or animal service worker.

1. What are two traits you should have if you are thinking of becoming a veterinarian?

   _____

   _____

2. What are examples of some things a vet does on the job?

   _____

   _____

3. What type of education do you need to become a vet?

   _____

   _____

4. Where do veterinarians work?

   _____

   _____

5. What are the duties of an animal technician and an animal service worker?

   _____

   _____

   _____

B. Use the Internet to research other possible career choices in this field and complete the chart.

Career	
Responsibilities	
Education Required	
Average Salary	
Is this a career you might pursue?	
Why or why not?	
Career	
Responsibilities	
Education Required	
Average Salary	
Is this a career you might pursue?	
Why or why not?	

Name _____ Date _____

A. Organize Your Ideas

Going Green
-
-
-

How can our individual actions affect our environment?	Why should we care about the state of resources a hundred years from now?	What are some things you presently do to positively impact the environment?
• • •	• • •	• • •

What else would you like to know about "going green"?

_____

_____

B. The Big Picture

Complete the graphic organizer by writing the passage topic and a key idea in each outside box. Then write a big idea in the center box.

"Smaller Steps, Better Impact"
Topic:
Key Idea:

"The Greener Life"
Topic:
Key Idea:

To me, "going green" means that . . .

One idea I'll take away with me is . . .

"Global Warming and Climate Change"
Topic:
Key Idea:

"Good-Bye, Fossil Fuels"
Topic:
Key Idea:

C. Expedition Dictionary

You will read the following vocabulary words throughout the Expedition. As you learn the words, use them as often as possible in your oral and written language.

"Smaller Steps, Better Impact"

prohibit   (v) *forbid by law or by an order*

hybrid   (n) *something that has two different parts performing essentially the same function*

efficient   (adj) *bringing about the wanted result using the least amount of time, materials, or effort*

response   (n) *something that is said or done in answer; a reply*

accumulation   (n) *the process of piling up, collecting, or gathering over a period of time*

significant   (adj) *very important*

"The Greener Life"

resources   (n) *things that are available to take care of a need*

ecology   (n) *the balance between people's lifestyles and the living things on Earth*

preserve   (v) *protect from harm or damage; keep in a certain condition*

environment   (n) *all the conditions surrounding plants, animals, and people that affect the health, growth, and development of those living things*

negligent   (adj) *being careless*

"Global Warming and Global Climate Change"

globe   (n) *Earth*

nature   (n) *everything in the physical world that is not made by human beings*

system   (n) *a group of things or parts working together or connected in such a way as to form a whole*

habitat   (n) *the place where an animal or plant is normally found*

theory   (n) *an explanation of how or why something happens*

contributes   (v) *has a part in bringing about*

"Good-Bye, Fossil Fuels"

depleted   (v) *reduced in number or quantity so as to endanger the ability to function*

crisis   (n) *a time of great danger or difficulty; anxiety about the future*

energy   (n) *the power of certain forces in nature to do work*

alternative   (adj) *allowing a choice between two or more things*

design   (n) *the particular plan that is followed to make something work*

Dictionary Challenge

Write a creative story about the life of a plastic water bottle using as many of the vocabulary words as possible.

Name _____   Date _____

Vocabulary

"Smaller Steps, Better Impact"

A. Put a check mark in each row to indicate how well you know each boldfaced word.

	Know This Word	Have Seen This Word	Don't Know This Word
prohibit (v) *forbid by law or by an order* The judge might *prohibit* the use of garbage barges.			
hybrid (n) *something that has two different parts performing essentially the same function* Her car is a *hybrid* that runs on fuel and electricity.			
efficient (adj) *bringing about the wanted result using the least amount of time, materials, or effort* An *efficient* car gets very good gas mileage on the road.			
response (n) *something that is said or done in answer; a reply* We need a quick *response* to the landfill problem because we need a place to dispose of our trash.			
accumulation (n) *the process of piling up, collecting, or gathering over a period of time* Everyone became upset about the *accumulation* of garbage at the city landfill.			
significant (adj) *very important* Recycling has made a *significant* impact on our environment.			

B. Read each statement. Circle true or false.

1. Everyone agrees that recycling is not a **significant** way to start "going green."   true   false

2. An **accumulation** of garbage in the house would be dirtier than a garbage bag.   true   false

3. Using recycled products is an **efficient** use of "Earth friendly" materials.   true   false

4. If your parents **prohibit** you from driving, they give you permission.   true   false

5. Citizens expect a **response** from city officials to an environmental problem.   true   false

6. If a new plant is a cross between a tomato and a carrot, it is a **hybrid**.   true   false

Name _____ Date _____

Word Building

A. Read the following definitions, then use words from the box to complete the chart. Look up word meanings in the dictionary to check your work.

allow	ban	effective	meaningful	notable	prevent
productive	restrict	streamlined	unimportant	vital	wasteful

Words	Definitions	Synonyms	Antonyms
significant	*very important*	1. 2. 3.	
prohibit	*forbid by law or by an order*	1. 2. 3.	
efficient	*bringing about the wanted result using the least amount of time, materials, or effort*	1. 2. 3.	

B. Write a sentence using each vocabulary word. Write a second sentence using a synonym or antonym as a context clue for the vocabulary word.

1. Sentence 1: _____

   _____

   Sentence 2: _____

   _____

2. Sentence 1: _____

   _____

   Sentence 2: _____

   _____

3. Sentence 1: _____

   _____

   Sentence 2: _____

   _____

Name _____ Date _____

Cause and Effect

Read each effect on the right side of the chart. Reread "Smaller Steps, Better Impact" to find causes that led to this effect. Write them below *Causes* in the chart.

Causes	Effect
Cars release carbon dioxide into the air.	Carbon dioxide accumulates in the atmosphere.
_____ release carbon dioxide into the air.	
_____ release carbon dioxide into the air.	

Causes	Effect
In 2005, marketing firms said	The Prius manufacturer made improvements to the Prius.
Other studies	
The Prius manufacturer evaluated	

Causes	Effect
If people drive	. . . the carbon footprint on Earth will be reduced.
If people _____ or ride	
If car manufacturing becomes	

Name _____   Date _____

Write in Response to Reading

A. Are you a green teen? Take this survey to find out.

1. I encourage my family to replace old lightbulbs with new energy-saving lightbulbs to reduce our carbon footprint.	☐ yes ☐ sometimes ☐ no
2. I would help start a recycling program for my school.	☐ yes ☐ maybe ☐ no
3. My school has a recycling program now. I am careful to put things that can be recycled in the recycling bins.	☐ yes ☐ sometimes ☐ no
4. I walk or bike to school.	☐ yes ☐ sometimes ☐ no
5. I turn off lights and electronic devices such as the computer or DVD player when I'm not using them.	☐ yes ☐ sometimes ☐ no
6. I take shorter or cooler showers because showers account for two-thirds of all water heating costs.	☐ yes ☐ sometimes ☐ no
7. I would organize or volunteer at a clean-up day for my school or neighborhood.	☐ yes ☐ maybe ☐ no

B. Imagine that your local power company is having a contest to determine the greenest teen. Write a letter to the president of the company explaining why you should win.

_____

_____

_____

_____

_____

_____

_____

_____

_____

_____

_____

_____

_____

_____

_____

_____

_____

Name _____   Date _____

Vocabulary

"The Greener Life"

A. Rate your knowledge of each boldfaced word.

   3   I know what this word means, and I can use it in a sentence.

   2   I have an idea of this word's meaning, but I need to know more.

   1   I don't know what this word means.

☐   **resources** (n) *things that are available to take care of a need*
The factory's pollution ruined one of the town's most important *resources*: the water in the lake.

☐   **ecology** (n) *the balance between people's lifestyles and the living things on Earth*
People who are aware of our *ecology* are learning better ways to take care of our planet.

☐   **preserve** (v) *protect from harm or damage; keep in a certain condition*
We should *preserve* the rain forest, not destroy it.

☐   **environment** (n) *all the conditions surrounding plants, animals, and people that affect the health, growth, and development of those living things*
When we reduce our amount of trash, we affect our *environment* in a good way.

☐   **negligent** (adj) *being careless*
I feel like I am *negligent* when I throw away perfectly good clothes that I could give to someone who needs them.

B. Complete each sentence with the correct vocabulary word from Part A.

1. People who throw trash in lakes are _____. They don't care about the environment.

2. Wind and sun are natural _____ that can produce energy.

3. Will city officials build houses on the open land, or will they _____ it?

4. People who recycle often do it to help the _____.

5. You study living things in biology class. When you study _____, you learn how living things interact.

Name _____   Date _____

Word Building

A. The following new words have *resource* or *preserve* as the base word and one or more word parts added. Circle the word parts that have been added to each word, then write a definition of the word. Check your definitions in the dictionary.

Inflectional Endings	-s	-ed			
Suffixes	-ful	-ly	-ness	-ation	-ist

New Words	Definitions
resource	*something that is available to take care of a need*
1. resources	
2. resourceful	
3. resourcefully	
4. resourcefulness	
preserve	*protect from harm; keep in a certain condition*
5. preserved	
6. preservation	
7. preservationist	

B. Use the BEST word from Part A to complete each sentence.

1. We must protect air and water because they are important _____.

2. I walk through the forest trails that are _____ for the public to enjoy.

3. My community voted for the _____ of a strip of land that connects two lakes.

4. When Elena was lost in the woods, she built a shelter. She kept warm and dry until someone found her. Elena is a _____ person.

5. Freegans continually find new, green ways to obtain what they need. They live _____.

6. John Muir helped protect the Yosemite Valley and other natural areas. He was a famous _____.

Name _____   Date _____

Cause and Effect

Complete the chart about "The Greener Life" by writing the effects that result from one cause.

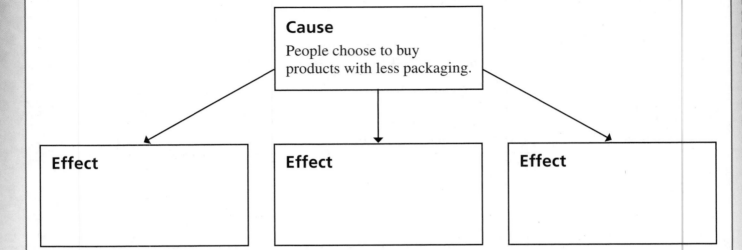

Cause
People choose to buy
products with less packaging.

Effect

Effect

Effect

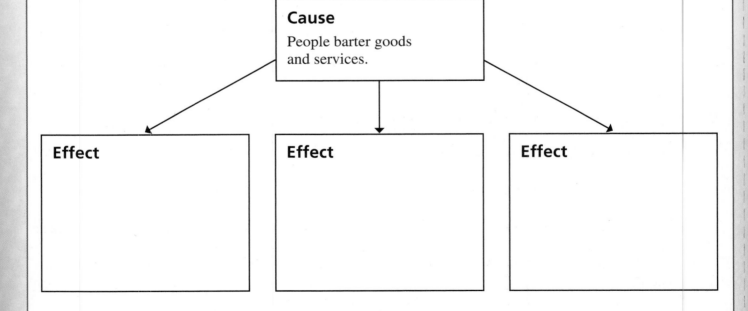

Cause
People barter goods
and services.

Effect

Effect

Effect

Name _____   **Date** _____

Write in Response to Reading

Your family has decided to become freegans. Decorate your room any way you would like, but you must use only materials that are reused or recycled. Describe what your room would look like and how you would use recycled materials to create furniture, storage, and art.

_____

_____

_____

_____

_____

_____

_____

_____

_____

_____

_____

_____

_____

_____

_____

_____

_____

_____

_____

_____

_____

_____

_____

_____

_____

_____

_____

Name _____   Date _____

Review Vocabulary

A. Replace each underlined word with a vocabulary word from "Smaller Steps, Better Impact" that is its antonym.

Organic and Fair-Trade Clothing

Becca and Timothy realize that their lifestyle choices have a 1. <u>minor</u> impact on the environment. They want to be a green family, so they 2. <u>allow</u> putting things in the trash if those materials could be reused or recycled. They use public transportation and reusable grocery bags to help make a(n) 3. <u>wasteful</u> use of energy and materials. They think of their impact on the air, water, animals, and other humans. They refuse to be 4. <u>attentive</u>. Becca and Timothy stay informed. They try to learn everything they can to 5. <u>harm</u> the environment.

---

1. _____   4. _____

2. _____   5. _____

3. _____

B. Write a word from the box that BEST completes each sentence.

hybrid	response	efficient	accumulation	preserve
ecology	resources	significant	environment	prohibit

1. Car exhaust and oil spills are forms of pollution that harm the _____.

2. We can reduce the _____ of garbage by recycling and reusing materials.

3. The president called for a quick _____ to the climate change problem.

4. We study _____ to learn how human actions affect other living things.

5. Unlike coal and gas, wind and solar power are energy _____ that are clean and won't run out.

6. Javier drives a _____; the engine can run on either electricity stored in the battery or traditional fuels.

Name _____ Date _____

Extend Vocabulary

A. Use your affixionary to help you complete the following chart.

neglect (v)	*to be* _____
negligent (adj)	*being careless*
negligence (n)	*the condition of* _____
negligible (adj)	*unimportant; not worth* _____
significant (adj)	*very important*
significance (n)	*the condition of* _____
significantly (adv)	*in an* _____
response (n)	*something said or done in answer; reply*
responsive (adj)	*quickly* _____
responsively (adv)	*done in* _____
respond (v)	*to* _____

B. Complete each sentence with one of the words from Part A.

1. The new recycling program _____ decreased the amount of trash in the city's landfill.

2. When people create waste, their actions affect Earth. Will future generations blame us for this _____ of the environment?

3. Olivia studied air and water pollution in a lake near her home. The pollution is not a small, or _____, problem.

4. Some land in our community is polluted with trash. A group of volunteers acted _____ to this environmental problem. They started a community garden project.

5. A boat's gas tank leaked gas into the lake. A county official determined the _____ of the spill.

6. How do you _____ when you see problems in your environment?

Name _____   Date _____

Assess Comprehension and Vocabulary

A. Read the following passage. Notice causes and their effects in the text. Remember that a *cause* is what made something happen and an *effect* is what happened.

> In cities everywhere, rooftop gardens are helping the environment. People have put vegetation on buildings since the ancient days of the Hanging Gardens of Babylon. Back then, they planted gardens for their beauty. Today, our reasons for planting these gardens are related to ecology. Have you ever seen satellite pictures of rooftops on Google Earth? You look down to see a lot of ugly concrete and tar. Tar on roads and rooftops soaks up heat from the sun. That means cities often are hotter than surrounding areas. One solution is a rooftop garden. On a hot day, garden roofs, or green roofs, can be cooler than other rooftops by 25–80°F. These rooftop gardens make temperatures inside the buildings cooler on hot days and warmer on cooler days. So, rooftop gardens make heating and cooling of buildings more efficient. After a rainstorm, water running into the sewers typically has an accumulation of pollutants from the city. Soil in a rooftop garden soaks up water, so fewer pollutants get into sewers. In a heavy rainstorm, rooftop soil can help prevent local floods. As you can see, rooftop gardens can have a significant impact on water systems.

B. Circle the letter of each correct answer.

1. In cities everywhere, rooftop gardens are helping the *environment*. Which phrase BEST replaces *environment*?

   A. new buildings and construction

   B. work people do

   C. conditions where people live and work

   D. harmful pollution

2. Which word does NOT go with *ecology*?

   A. balance

   B. separate

   C. lifestyle

   D. living things

3. Which word is an antonym for *efficient*?

   A. wise

   B. useful

   C. effective

   D. wasteful

4. Which word is a synonym for *significant*?

   A. minor

   B. unnecessary

   C. important

   D. small

Name _____   Date _____

5. Which word is a synonym for *accumulation*?

   A. collection

   B. scattering

   C. vacancy

   D. consumption

6. What is the topic of this passage?

   A. city water supplies

   B. Hanging Gardens of Babylon

   C. rooftop gardens

   D. city weather

7. Which of the following would be the BEST title for this passage?

   A. How to Build Rooftop Gardens

   B. The Benefits of Green Rooftops

   C. Local Flood Prevention

   D. Energy Efficient Buildings

8. In ancient days, people planted gardens on buildings . . .

   A. to shade their homes from sunlight.

   B. because they looked beautiful.

   C. so it didn't get too hot in the summer.

   D. to keep sewers from getting too full.

9. Which of the following is an effect of rooftop gardening?

   A. It reduces energy for cooling a building.

   B. It makes cities hotter in summer.

   C. It increases local flooding.

   D. It adds dirt and pollution to the city.

10. Which effect does a tar rooftop have on the environment?

    A. It keeps the building cooler on hot days.

    B. It provides a place for pigeons to flock.

    C. It leaks during heavy rains.

    D. It makes the outdoor temperature warmer.

11. What causes rooftop gardens to have a significant impact on a city water system?

    A. Polluted rainwater runs into the city sewers.

    B. Workers use up large amounts of water for the plants on the roof.

    C. Soil in a rooftop garden soaks up some rainwater and keeps some of it out of sewers.

    D. Rooftop gardens cool buildings more efficiently.

12. What is the effect of rooftop gardens when a city has heavy rain?

    A. Soil gets into the water systems.

    B. Fewer pollutants get into sewers.

    C. The gardens flood and die.

    D. The sewers overflow.

13. How do rooftop gardens help prevent local floods?

    A. The garden soil soaks up some rainwater.

    B. The plants absorb all the rain.

    C. Rain collects in pots on the roofs.

    D. The cooler air prevents rainy weather.

Name _____   Date _____

14. Read the following statement. What are two causes?

    More buildings may have rooftop gardens in the future.

    _____

    _____

    _____

    _____

    _____

    _____

    _____

15. Read the following fact. What are the effects on people and the environment? Identify four effects.

    Rooftop gardens protect a building from extreme temperatures.

    _____

    _____

    _____

    _____

    _____

    _____

    _____

    _____

Name _____   Date _____

Reteach

A. Read the following passage. Circle four causes that lead to the effect of polar bears drowning.

More and more polar bears in Antarctica are drowning. What could cause such a tragedy? Researchers and ecologists have stepped in to figure that out. They have found that accumulation of carbon dioxide in the atmosphere has increased. The carbon dioxide causes Earth's temperature to rise. Warmer weather means that a lot of Earth's polar ice is melting. Polar bears usually stay on floating ice sheets as they hunt for fish in the ocean. The distances between the ice sheets are growing larger. Sometimes the bears have to swim up to 60 miles to reach the next ice sheet. Even though they are very strong swimmers, long swims like this exhaust the bears. The sea waves often overtake them.

B. Read the following passage, then answer the questions.

The Dead Sea is dying! What does that mean? Here's the answer. The Dead Sea is in a desert area of the Middle East. It is one of the world's saltiest bodies of water. It's so salty that it cannot sustain life. Now do you understand its name? In recent years, the Dead Sea has been drying up. Waters from the Jordan River used to flow into the Dead Sea. Now the Jordan River is just a trickle where it joins the Dead Sea. The people in Israel, Jordan, and Syria have used the river water for drinking and irrigating their desert crops. The level of the Dead Sea has been dropping at a rate of a yard a year. One-third of it has already disappeared. Twenty years ago, a spa opened on the shore of the waters. Now the shoreline is almost a mile away. What could save the Dead Sea? One plan involves moving water from the Red Sea to the Dead Sea. Canals and pipelines would have to be constructed for this huge project. Environmentalists warn that the plan will change the mineral balance in the water.

Name _____   Date _____

It is impossible for creatures to live in the Dead Sea. What is the cause?

The water _____.

Identify three effects that result from the cause. Use information from the passage, your answers, and what you know to complete the diagram.

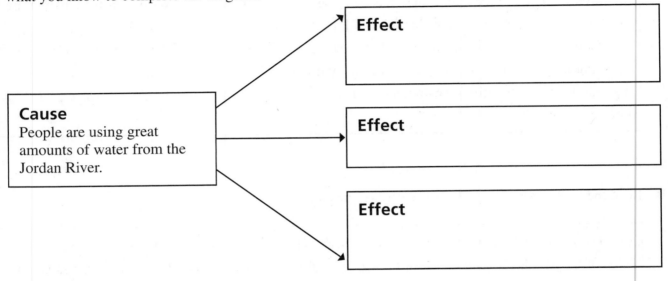

Cause
People are using great amounts of water from the Jordan River.

Effect

Effect

Effect

What are two possible effects of the plan to bring water from the Red Sea to the Dead Sea?

One possible effect is that _____.

Another possible effect is that _____.

Name _____ Date _____

Natural Food Marketplace

Information to Help You Make a Wise Purchasing Decision about GMOs

What Are Genetically Modified Foods?

Genetically modified foods—also known as GM foods, GMOs (genetically modified organisms), or genetically engineered foods—are foods that have been altered using modern science techniques. These include foods made for humans or animals. In the laboratory, scientists alter the genes, or basic biological structure, of plants. They create crops with desired traits, such as resistance to disease, insects, or drought. The theory is that by using genetic modification, people will be able to create foods that are hardier and can grow in more locations. This will help feed growing populations around the globe.

Are GM Foods Common?

Today, more than 40 genetically modified plant varieties have been approved by the U.S. government. These include some kinds of cantaloupes, corn, tomatoes, soybeans, and beets. Most processed foods, such as crackers and cereals, already have at least some traces of GM foods.

Are GM Foods Safe?

The U.S. government and groups throughout the world support the process of genetic modification. They claim the system will prevent a food-shortage crisis that could occur as the global population increases. However, many scientists, government officials, environmental groups, and consumers are concerned about possible hazards—global and personal—connected with GM foods. Plants in the same habitat may be affected and altered by GM crops. Animals that feed on these plants may be harmed. Another concern is that GM plants may crossbreed with weed plants in the same habitat creating "super weeds." A hazard for consumers is that GM foods may contribute to the development of food allergies. GM foods also may pose unknown health risks because the food's genetic structure is altered.

Our Policy Statement

We recognize the long-term effects of GM foods to the environment and to individuals are not fully known. We, at Natural Food Marketplace, are taking action to sell foods that have not been genetically modified and do not include GM ingredients. For all of our name-brand products, we seek sources that provide us with all-natural, non-genetically modified ingredients. As part of our policy, we encourage our suppliers to explore ways to help us meet this goal now and in the future.

We also support organic agriculture. Buying organic food is an alternative that helps assure consumers that the food has no preservatives, additives, or GM ingredients. By law, organic foods cannot contain GM ingredients or be grown from genetically engineered seeds.

We believe that by supplying organic foods and providing alternative foods with no GM ingredients, our market contributes to the health and well-being of our customers. Because no one knows for certain what the long-term effects of genetic engineering might be, we suggest people purchase wholesome and natural foods.

Name _____   **Date** _____

Exploring Careers: Refuse Worker

A. Answer the following questions about a career as a refuse worker.

1. What education do most refuse workers have?

   _____

2. Name three abilities a refuse worker needs.

   _____

   _____

3. What is a typical income for a refuse worker?

   _____

4. What are three different tasks that a refuse worker might do on the job?

   _____

   _____

   _____

5. How might a job as a refuse worker be rewarding?

   _____

   _____

   _____

B. Use the Internet to research other possible career choices in this field and complete the chart.	
Career	
Responsibilities	
Education Required	
Average Salary	
Is this a career you might pursue?	
Why or why not?	
Career	
Responsibilities	
Education Required	
Average Salary	
Is this a career you might pursue?	
Why or why not?	

Name _____   Date _____

Vocabulary

"Global Warming and Global Climate Change"

A. Write one or more numbers next to each boldfaced word to show when you have seen, heard, or used this word.

5   I use it in everyday conversation.
4   I heard it on TV or on the radio.
3   I heard or used it in school.
2   I read it in a book, magazine, or online.
1   I have not read, heard, or used this word.

☐   **globe** (n) *Earth*
Changing weather patterns seem to be happening all over the *globe* from China to Mexico.

☐   **nature** (n) *everything in the physical world that is not made by human beings*
Many people enjoy being outdoors in *nature*.

☐   **system** (n) *a group of things or parts working together or connected in such a way as to form a whole*
Algae are part of a *system* in the natural world that produces oxygen.

☐   **habitat** (n) *the place where an animal or plant is normally found*
The *habitat* of polar bears is sea ice, which is basically a giant iceberg.

☐   **theory** (n) *an explanation of how or why something happens*
Many people disagree about the *theory* of global warming because they can't agree on what is causing the rise in temperature.

☐   **contributes** (v) *has a part in bringing about*
Recycling *contributes* to our community's effort to go green.

B. Complete each sentence with the correct vocabulary word from Part A.

1. Some biologists are proving the _____ that people who live in a green way are happier and healthier.

2. Forests, rivers, deserts, and oceans are all part of _____.

3. Do you think that carbon dioxide _____ to global warming?

4. The ocean is the _____ of a whale.

5. Satellite signals can travel around the _____.

6. A recycling bin, a plan for reusing and bartering, and a list of recycled products are parts of a home recycling _____.

Name _____ Date _____

Big Picture Notes

Notes about _____	Questions _____

Summary

Name _____   Date _____

Word Building

A. One or more word parts from the box have been added to build new words that have the base word *nature*, *system*, or *theory*. Circle the word parts that were added in the new words, then write the definitions.

Inflectional Ending	-s	-ies		
Prefix	un-			
Suffix	-atic	-ist	-al	-ize

New Words	Definitions
nature	*everything in the physical world that is not made by human beings*
1. natural	
2. unnatural	
3. naturalists	
system	*a group of things or parts working together or connected in such a way as to form a whole*
4. systems	
5. systematic	
6. unsystematic	
theory	*an explanation of how or why something happens*
7. theories	
8. theorize	
9. theorist	

B. Read the paragraph, then choose from the new words in Part A to complete each sentence.

Scientists have different _____ about why Earth's temperature is rising. Scientists conduct studies in a _____ way. No one believed the results of one study because it was conducted in an _____ way. The students listened to one _____ who gave different explanations for global warming. Some scientists think the rise in global temperatures is part of a _____ cycle. Other scientists think the rapid rise in yearly temperatures is _____.

Name _____   Date _____

Write in Response to Reading

A. What can individuals, communities, corporations, and the government do about global warming? Brainstorm ideas and write them in each category.

Individuals	Communities	Corporations	Government

B. Create a rap, a poem, or song lyrics that tell different ways people can care for the environment.

_____
_____
_____
_____
_____
_____
_____
_____
_____
_____
_____
_____
_____
_____
_____
_____
_____
_____
_____

Name _____   Date _____

Vocabulary

"Good-Bye, Fossil Fuels"

A. Put a check mark in each row to indicate how well you know each boldfaced word.

	Know This Word	Have Seen This Word	Don't Know This Word
depleted (v) *reduced in number or quantity so as to endanger the ability to function* If our natural fuel resources are *depleted*, we will have a problem producing energy.			
crisis (n) *a time of great danger or difficulty; anxiety about the future* Many people worry about the *crisis* of world pollution.			
energy (n) *the power of certain forces in nature to do work* We have many different forms of *energy* available to us in the land, water, and air.			
alternative (adj) *allowing a choice between two or more things* If using gasoline is a problem, we need to find *alternative* ways to fuel our cars.			
design (n) *the particular plan that is followed to make something work* We chose the *design* that used solar panels for energy for our science project.			

B. Choose the ending that BEST completes each sentence.

use other fuels   others say it will not cause great harm   comes from a battery
source of energy   the best plan in the science fair

1. The judges said our **design** for a solar oven was _____.

2. The **energy** needed to power my camera _____.

3. Wind turbines are an **alternative** _____.

4. Once our oil supply is **depleted**, we will have to _____.

5. Some people say that climate change is a **crisis**, but _____
_____.

Name _____   Date _____

Word Building

A. The word *alternative* means "allowing a choice." The Latin root *alter* means "other." The prefix *de-* can change the meaning of the base word to its opposite. Read the following words and definitions.

Words	Definitions	Words	Definitions
alter (v)	*change*	**defrost** (v)	*remove frost or ice; thaw*
alternate (v)	*go back and forth from one thing to another*	**deactivate** (v)	*make inactive, or not active*
alternative (adj)	*allowing a choice*	**decode** (v)	*translate code into ordinary language*
alterable (adj)	*able to be altered or changed*	**deplete** (v)	*reduce so as to endanger the ability to function*
alteration (n)	*a change; a modification*	**decompose** (v)	*rot or decay*

B. Complete each sentence with one of the words from Part A.

1. Sunlight is an _____ source of energy for electricity.

2. We will have to stop hiking if we _____ our supply of water.

3. Lao tried to _____ the strange message so he could understand it.

4. Mrs. Servo's decision is final. It is not _____.

5. The building supervisor had to _____ the security alarm before people entered the office each morning.

6. The play director made one _____ during the last rehearsal because we couldn't hear Javier say his line.

7. Before the cook grilled the frozen meat, he had to _____ it.

8. Mom decided to _____ between the two fruits the children liked to eat.

9. The witness to the crime repeated his story. He did not _____ one fact.

10. Dead plants began to _____ on the forest floor.

Name _____ Date _____

Compare and Contrast

A. Use information from "Good-Bye, Fossil Fuels" to write facts about nuclear power and wind power in the chart. Some parts of the chart are done for you.

Features	Nuclear Power	Wind Power
Energy Source		
Depends on Fossil Fuels?	no	
Location		
Equipment Needed	nuclear reactor	
Waste		no waste
Disadvantages		
Problems to Be Solved	how to dispose of waste safely	adding battery power to operate the turbine when wind is low

B. Read the completed chart. Complete the following statements to compare and contrast the two types of power plants. Use signal words or phrases from the box. In your sentences, circle the signal words and phrases you used.

like	similar to	also	as well as	both
on the other hand	although	unlike	but	

1. Compare: Nuclear and wind power _____

   _____

2. Contrast: Nuclear power _____

   _____

   _____ wind power _____

   _____

Name _____   Date _____

Write in Response to Reading

A. Global warming can cause harm to Earth. Some say disasters can occur. How would you warn the world about these doomsday scenarios? Create a warning poster.

B. Imagine you live in a perfect green city or town. Write a description of your location. Brag about how your community gets it power and how the buses, trains, and automobiles operate. Why is it better than other communities?

_____

_____

_____

_____

_____

_____

_____

_____

_____

_____

_____

_____

Name _____   Date _____

Review Vocabulary

A. For each underlined word or phrase, write a synonym from the words in the box.

globe	nature	system	habitat	depleted	crisis

1. The polar ice caps where polar bears live are melting, so the <u>home</u> of polar bears is disappearing.

    _____

2. Nonrenewable resources like fossil fuels can be <u>greatly reduced</u>, but wind and solar energy cannot be used up. _____

3. Some factories next to rivers dump pollutants into the waters. They cause harm to <u>living things outdoors</u>. _____

4. As human beings, we are part of a <u>thing that interacts</u> that affects our environment.

    _____

5. If global warming can cause flooding or famine, the world could face a <u>major problem</u>.

    _____

6. The atmosphere around the <u>Earth</u> traps the heat of the sun. _____

B. Circle the word that BEST completes each sentence.

Modern architects are planning buildings that use (alternative, abrupt) sources of power. When architects plan a building, they add solar panels and wind turbines in their (emission, design). The sun and wind provide renewable sources of (habitat, energy). People argue about global warming. They say this (theory, system) has not been proved. However, scientists believe that fossil fuels (coincide, contribute) to rising temperatures. Eco-friendly architects are discovering new ways to use fewer sources of fossil fuel.

Name _____   Date _____

Extend Vocabulary

A. The word *biofuel* uses the Greek root *bio*, meaning "life." Read the following words and their meanings. Notice how all the word meanings connect to the word *life*.

Words	Definitions
biofuels (n)	*fuels made from living matter*
biology (n)	*the science of life*
biodegradable (adj)	*capable of being decomposed by bacteria or other living organisms; eco-friendly material*
biodiversity (n)	*the variety of living things in an ecosystem*
biosphere (n)	*all parts of Earth and its atmosphere that have life*
biography (n)	*someone's life story written by another person*

B. Choose the word from Part A that BEST completes each sentence. Think about the meanings of the words and how you have heard each word used.

1. Washing clothes with _____ soap will not harm the environment.

2. We need to protect and preserve all the plants and animals in Earth's _____.

3. Maria read a _____ of Al Gore, the former vice president who made a movie about global warming.

4. Many plants and animals rely on the coral reef for shelter. The coral reef supports much _____.

5. Fiona learned how plants use sunlight and carbon dioxide in _____ class.

6. In the future, your car may not use gas, which comes from nonrenewable energy. Your car may run on _____, which come from corn or other renewable sources.

C. Write two sentences. Choose a word from Part A to use in each sentence.

1. _____

2. _____

Name _____   Date _____

Assess Comprehension and Vocabulary

A. Read the passage. Make comparisons and contrasts about details that are similar and different.

When people needed a cleaner source of energy, they used hydropower. For example, the air around the dams that produce hydroelectric power is cleaner than the air around a coal processing plant. The largest hydroelectric dam in the United States is the Grand Coulee Dam in Washington. It provides a great benefit to farmers. The dam is part of an irrigation system for agriculture in central Washington. Despite the benefits, the dam has caused some problems to nature in the surrounding area. The dam blocked salmon and steelhead fish from accessing their habitat on the upper Columbia River. The lifestyles of local Native American tribes were centered on fishing. The dam permanently obstructed their fishing grounds. Also, flooding caused by the dam forced Native Americans to relocate their settlements.

The Three Gorges Dam on the Yangtze River in China is the largest hydroelectric dam in the world. It also has caused much controversy. Millions of local residents have been forced to relocate because of flooding. Another effect is that the Yangtze River dolphin is now extinct. The dam also has begun to contribute to increased flooding and landslides along the river shores.

B. Circle the letter of each correct answer.

1. Which word is a synonym for *energy*?
   A. emission
   B. power
   C. anxiety
   D. atom

2. Which of the following does NOT go with the word *system*?
   A. organized
   B. networked
   C. working together
   D. disconnected

3. Which word is NOT a synonym for *nature*?
   A. wildlife
   B. outdoors
   C. pollutants
   D. plants

4. Which word is NOT a synonym for *habitat*?
   A. surroundings
   B. system
   C. environment
   D. home

Name _____   Date _____

5. Choose the phrase that BEST restates what
   contribute means in this sentence.
   The dam also has begun to contribute to
   increased flooding and landslides.
   A. cause to happen
   B. decide the reason for
   C. invent
   D. be a theory for

6. What is the topic of this passage?
   A. the Three Gorges Dam
   B. how hydropower works
   C. effects of hydroelectric dams
   D. groups that oppose dams

7. Which of the following would be a good title
   for this passage?
   A. Hydropower: Good Idea or Bad Idea?
   B. Rivers and Clean Energy
   C. Local Floods: Causes and Prevention
   D. Changing Habitat, Changing Species

8. What is one good effect of the Grand Coulee
   Dam?
   A. It helps make salmon fishing easier.
   B. It helps irrigate farmland.
   C. It prevents local floods.
   D. It became the largest dam in the United
      States.

9. The Columbia and Yangtze Rivers both have
   dams. Which effect happened at both dams?
   A. The river dolphin became extinct.
   B. The habitat of the wildlife changed.
   C. Landslides increased along the shores.
   D. The salmon and steelhead disappeared.

10. Which statement applies only to the Grand
    Coulee Dam?
    A. It has caused local people to move.
    B. It has caused landslides.
    C. It produces hydroelectric power.
    D. It is part of an irrigation system.

11. What do the Grand Coulee and the Three
    Gorges Dams have in common?
    A. They obstruct salmon fishing grounds.
    B. They are hydroelectric.
    C. They irrigate agriculture.
    D. They only have positive effects.

12. Which statement applies only to the Three
    Gorges Dam?
    A. It is part of an irrigation system.
    B. It threatened Native American culture.
    C. It has caused landslides.
    D. It has caused flooding.

13. Which effects did both dams cause?
    A. The native fishing culture was destroyed.
    B. Fish species became extinct.
    C. Local people were forced to relocate.
    D. Farmers could grow crops in the desert.

Name _____ **Date** _____

14. Which of the following is a benefit of both dams?

    A. They provide a clean source of energy.

    B. They irrigate local agriculture.

    C. They prevent local floods.

    D. They provide a cleaner habitat for fish.

15. Summarize the similarities between the Grand Coulee Dam and the Three Gorges Dam. Include four ways they are similar.

    _____

    _____

    _____

    _____

    _____

    _____

Name _____ Date _____

Reteach

Read the passages. For each passage, compare similarities and contrast differences. Answer the questions.

The Arctic and Louisiana

Changing landscapes threaten the survival of the cultures. The Arctic ice is thawing. This is disrupting the way of life of the Inuit and Sami people who live there. Similarly, in southeastern Louisiana, the sinking coastline at the joint of the Mississippi River and the Gulf of Mexico threatens the Cajun lifestyle. The lifestyles of both cultures are at risk.

---

1. What are facts about the Arctic? _____

_____

2. What are facts about Louisiana? _____

_____

3. What is different about the two places? _____

_____

4. What is similar about them? _____

_____

5. What do you know now? Complete the statement.
   When the environment changes, _____.

Reasons for Erosion

Coastal erosion is happening in both the Arctic and in Louisiana. In other words, the land on the shore is sinking underwater. However, the causes are very different. In the Arctic, the rising temperatures cause the ice to melt. Arctic land is made up of permafrost, or constantly frozen soil and rock. When permafrost melts, the ground becomes soggy and flooded. In Louisiana, levees, or steep river embankments, have caused the land erosion. In the 1930s, levees were built to prevent flooding on the banks of the Mississippi. However, the levees prevent the river from carrying sediment and depositing it at the Louisiana coast. The coastline had depended on this natural maintenance.

Name _____   Date _____

6. What is the same about both places? _____

7. What are causes of erosion in the Arctic? _____

8. What are causes of erosion in Louisiana? _____

9. What do you know now? Complete the statement.
    When humans build structures like levees, _____
    _____.

Industries in the Arctic and Louisiana

Workers drill for oil off the shores of both the Arctic and Louisiana. Oil spills threaten the health and cleanliness of the environment. People fish in the Arctic and work in shrimping in Louisiana. Fishing in the Artic is important to the economy of the area. The oil spills in the region have threatened this important industry because fish are killed. The shrimping industry has been at the center of the Cajun lifestyle and diet for generations. Salt water from the gulf has flooded and killed wetlands and marshes, the habitats for wildlife and fish. The shrimp are not growing as large because of the loss of marshes where they would stay and grow before going out to the gulf.

---

10. Are the effects of the oil industries mostly the same or different in both places? Explain.
     _____
     _____
     _____

11. What is the same about the oil industry and fishing and shrimping? _____
     _____

12. What is different about what is happening to Arctic fish and Louisiana shrimp? _____
     _____
     _____

Name _____ Date _____

Real World—Flyer

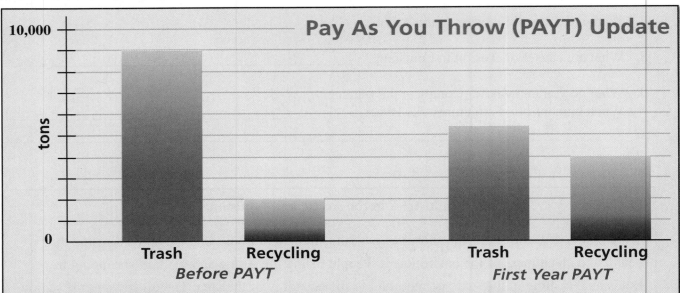

Municipal Waste Reduction and Recycling Program
Recycle: Save resources. Protect the environment.

Progress Report

During the past year, the response of ecologically mindful citizens to the improved recycling program has resulted in a significant increase in recycling and a decrease in trash. (See graph.) The weekly recycling pickup has prevented the accumulation of huge amounts of recycling that occurred in past years with the monthly plan. The decrease in trash has resulted in benefits to the local environment, including less trash sent to landfills.

Recycling Information

This information applies to all residents with municipal trash collection. In the current single-stream curbside recycling program, you do not have to separate paper from containers because modern techniques are very efficient at sorting materials at the recycling center.

Please rinse all containers, recycle only clean paper, and place all recycling items in your recycling container or a 30-gallon barrel clearly marked *Recycling*. Place newspapers and magazines in brown bags.

Paper
- Newspaper, magazines, catalogs, brown bags
- Paperback books, hardcover books with covers removed
- Office paper, fax paper, junk mail envelopes
- Paperboard from cereal boxes, cracker boxes
- Cardboard (maximum size 3' x 3')

Containers
- Glass bottles and jars
- Beverage cans, tin/steel cans and lids
- Aluminum, aluminum foil, pie plates
- All plastic marked with the following numbers: 1, 2, 3, 4, 5, 6, 7

The following items are prohibited: wax paper, paper towels, napkins, tissues, motor oil, and chemical containers. Also prohibited are cardboard that has been contaminated by food, such as pizza boxes, and plastic laminated paper, such as juice or milk boxes.

On another sheet of paper, make your own recycling "fact sheet" using information from the pamphlet. List how to and what to recycle. Check your facts with a partner.

Name _____   Date _____

Exploring Careers: Farmer

A. Answer the following questions about a career as a farmer.

1. Name four different kinds of farmers.

   _____

2. What is hydroponics?

   _____

   _____

3. What kind of work ethic does it take to be a farmer?

   _____

   _____

4. What education is helpful for farmers?

   _____

   _____

5. What is the average annual salary of a farm manager?

   _____

B. Use the Internet to research other possible career choices in this field and complete the chart.

Career	
Responsibilities	
Education Required	
Average Salary	
Is this a career you might pursue?	
Why or why not?	
Career	
Responsibilities	
Education Required	
Average Salary	
Is this a career you might pursue?	
Why or why not?	

Name _____   Date _____

A. Organize Your Ideas

Just for the Sport of It

-
-
-

How do sports bring people together?

-
-
-

Why are sports, especially violent ones, so popular in the United States?

-
-
-

Why do you think winning is so important that people will go to extreme lengths to be the best?

-
-
-

What else do you want to know about sports and what people do to win?

_____

_____

B. The Big Picture

Write the big idea of each passage in the outside ovals. Connect the passages in the center oval by writing the big picture.

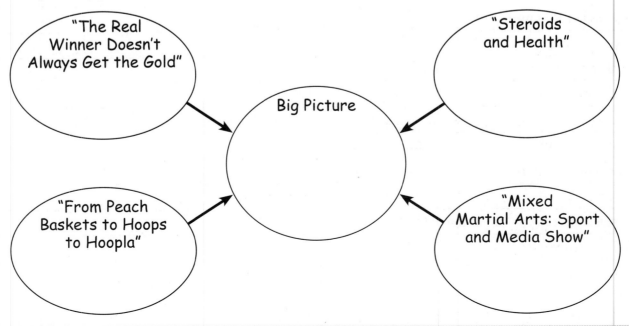

"The Real Winner Doesn't Always Get the Gold"

"Steroids and Health"

Big Picture

"From Peach Baskets to Hoops to Hoopla"

"Mixed Martial Arts: Sport and Media Show"

C. Expedition Dictionary

You will read the following vocabulary words throughout the Expedition. As you learn the words, use them as often as possible in your oral and written language.

"The Real Winner Doesn't Always Get the Gold"

assembled	(v) *gathered together in one place*
symbol	(n) *an object that represents something else*
compete	(v) *try hard to outdo others in a contest*
tolerance	(n) *acceptance and respect of others and their beliefs*
expert	(adj) *very skilled at something*
ideal	(adj) *perfect; very suitable*

"From Peach Baskets to Hoops to Hoopla"

benefit	(v) *get an advantage from something; be helped by something*
opposed	(v) *went against something; competed*
motion	(n) *movement*
transition	(n) *a change from one way to another*
media	(n) *the system or people through which information is communicated to society*
urban	(adj) *to do with the city*

"Steroids and Health"

speculate	(v) *wonder or guess about something without knowing all the facts*
chemicals	(n) *substances formed when two or more other substances act upon one another*
organic	(adj) *made using only natural products*
synthesized	(v) *produced a substance by a chemical or biological process*
soluble	(adj) *can be dissolved in liquid*
effects	(n) *the results or consequences of something*

"Mixed Martial Arts: Sport and Media Show"

competent	(adj) *having the skill or ability to do something well*
endeavors	(v) *tries very hard to do something*
maneuvers	(n) *difficult movements that require planning and skill*
vary	(v) *be different*
adhere	(v) *stick with an idea, plan, or rules*
spectacle	(n) *a remarkable and dramatic sight*

Dictionary Challenge

Write a letter of admiration to an athlete with whom you are familiar. Use as many vocabulary words as possible.

Name _____   Date _____

Vocabulary

"The Real Winner Doesn't Always Get the Gold"

A. Rate your knowledge of each boldfaced word.

3   familiar
2   somewhat familiar
1   unknown word

☐   **assembled** (v) *gathered together in one place*
    The players *assembled* at midcourt to discuss the rules of the game.

☐   **symbol** (n) *an object that represents something else*
    The five colorful rings linked together are the *symbol* of the Olympic Games.

☐   **compete** (v) *try hard to outdo others in a contest*
    Americans *compete* against each other to determine who goes to the Olympics.

☐   **tolerance** (n) *acceptance and respect of others and their beliefs*
    Athletes shake hands with people of other nations to demonstrate a *tolerance* of one another.

☐   **expert** (adj) *very skilled at something*
    Only *expert* cyclists make it to the Olympic Games.

☐   **ideal** (adj) *perfect; very suitable*
    The *ideal* athlete is someone with talent and the desire to work hard.

B. Read each statement. Circle true or false.

1. If all the students **assembled**, they went to different rooms.   true   false

2. A trophy is a **symbol** of losing a contest.   true   false

3. You **compete** against another team in a hockey game.   true   false

4. People express **tolerance** through anger and hatred.   true   false

5. An **expert** coach knows how to lead a team to a championship.   true   false

6. In an **ideal** season, your favorite team would win every game.   true   false

Name _____ Date _____

Word Building

A. Some word endings, or suffixes, can change the part of speech of a word. The suffixes *-ance* and *-ence* can change some verbs into nouns. Complete the chart with the appropriate words or definitions.

Verbs	Definitions
appear	*look a certain way*
resist	*oppose somebody or something*
allow	*let someone have something*

+ *-ance*

Nouns	Definitions
	the way something looks or seems to other people
	a state of opposition to somebody or something
allowance	

Verbs	Definitions
reside	*live in a house, apartment, or other dwelling*
differ	*disagree*
depend	*rely on somebody or something*
confide	*tell someone a secret or private information*

+ *-ence*

Nouns	Definitions
residence	
difference	
	reliance on someone for help or support
	a secret or private piece of information

B. Choose a verb or noun from Part A to complete each sentence.

1. I'm watching the cyclists in the race. They _____ to be strong and fast.

2. The runner fell down, got up, and continued racing. She always will _____ the idea of giving up.

3. Athletes often _____ on one another for support and motivation.

4. The U.S. Olympic team stays together in one _____ when the athletes are competing.

5. The United States raises funds for its Olympic team and gives each athlete an _____ of money to spend during competitions.

6. Occasionally, a referee and a coach may have a _____ of opinion regarding a penalty call.

Name _____ Date _____

Make Connections

Think about how the passage "The Real Winner Doesn't Always Get the Gold" is similar to your life, other texts you have read, and the world.

Describe what happens in the Innsbruck, Austria, 1964 section.	I connect this with my life because . . .
	This reminds me of a book, article, or movie because . . .
	I can connect this to the world because . . .

Describe what happens in the Seoul, South Korea, 1988 section.	In my own life, this reminds me of . . .
	I connect this to a book or article I read about . . .
	A real-world connection I would make is . . .

Name _____ Date _____

Write in Response to Reading

A. Long, Monti, Lemieux, Nishida, and Oe did selfless and courageous acts. Write your own story about a "real winner." Tell how an athlete sacrifices to perform a similar act. Choose a sport and create your own characters and plot. The setting is your school or community.

_____

_____

_____

_____

_____

_____

_____

_____

_____

_____

_____

_____

B. Imagine it is after the 1936 Olympics. Adolf Hitler has ordered Luz Long to explain why he helped Jesse Owens. Write what you imagine the conversation would be.

Hitler: You disobeyed my order that _____

Long: _____

_____

Hitler: _____

_____

Long: _____

_____

Hitler: _____

_____

Long: _____

_____

Hitler: _____

_____

Long: _____

_____

Name _____   Date _____

Vocabulary

"From Peach Baskets to Hoops to Hoopla"

A. Put a check mark in each row to indicate how well you know each boldfaced word.

	Know This Word	Have Seen This Word	Don't Know This Word
benefit (v) *get an advantage from something; be helped by something* The team was able to *benefit* from the extra day of rest.			
opposed (v) *went against something; competed* The crosstown rivals *opposed* each other in the basketball finals.			
motion (n) *movement* The *motion* of the ball was so quick it was hard to follow.			
transition (n) *a change from one way to another* Basketball had undergone a *transition* to the much different streetball.			
media (n) *the system or people through which information is communicated to society* Television is the most popular form of *media* for people to learn about streetball.			
urban (adj) *to do with the city* In Chicago, many *urban* youth organizations help keep young people off the streets.			

B. Choose the vocabulary word from Part A that BEST completes each sentence.

1. My friend and I _____ each other in a game of one-on-one.

2. You see a lot of advertising when you watch, read about, or listen to sports on television and other popular _____.

3. The coach demonstrated the arm _____ for blocking a shot.

4. Regular practices and a winning attitude will _____ your team.

5. He thinks it is difficult to make the _____ from high school to college.

6. Basketball is a popular sport in both rural and _____ areas.

Name _____   Date _____

Sequence

Examine the following photo. Think about the scene. You see one event. What other actions or events might have led to this one? Answer the questions to determine the sequence of events.

1. What is happening in the photo?

   _____

   _____

   _____

   _____

2. Name three events that could lead up to this one.

   _____

   _____

   _____

   _____

   _____

3. Read the events you wrote. Put them in sequence. The sequence will be in order of time from first to last. Add other events that make sense in the sequence.

   _____

   _____

   _____

   _____

4. Write two events that follow the event in the photo.

   _____

   _____

   _____

5. Write a summary. Use the events you listed. Use words like *first, then, next,* and *finally* to signal the chronology, or time sequence, of events.

   _____

   _____

   _____

   _____

Name _____   Date _____

Word Building

A. Use affixes to build on vocabulary words. Review the definitions of the boldfaced words on page 196. Use your affixionary to define new words.

		New Words	Definitions
sub- +	**urban**		
urban	+ *-ize*		
benefit	+ *-ial*		
un- +	**opposed**		
oppose	+ *-tion*		
transition	+ *-al*		

	New Words	Definitions
+ *-tion*		

	New Words	Definitions
+ *-al*		

B. Complete each sentence with one of the new words from Part A.

1. The _____ of the small town brought bigger stadiums and a professional team.

2. I was in _____ to athletes using steroids.

3. Moving from karate to kickboxing was _____ for both competitors.

4. The football player thought steroids were _____, but they ended up damaging his organs.

5. I didn't even have to run my best to win the race because I was _____.

Name _____   **Date** _____

Sequence

A. Review the passage "From Peach Baskets to Hoops to Hoopla." Complete the timeline with dates and events from the passage. Write a title for the timeline.

Title: _____

1891 _____

_____

_____   Lew Allen makes a wire basket.

_____   First women's basketball game takes place.

1894 _____

_____

1895 _____

1927 _____

1932 _____

_____   Basketball is introduced at the Berlin Olympics.

1946 _____

1949 _____

_____

_____   The Street Basketball Association is formed.

B. How did basketball change from its beginning to today? Use signal words to describe the sequence of events.

Basketball first began _____

_____

_____

_____

_____

_____

_____

Name _____   Date _____

Write in Response to Reading

A. Read about flopping, then imagine you are a flopper. Write a brief article defending your actions, titled "Confessions of an NBA Flopper."

What Is a Flop?

In basketball, a flop is when a defensive player intentionally falls to the floor after slight physical contact with another player. Floppers want officials to see the fall and believe the offensive player knocked him or her down on purpose. Then, the official will call a charging foul against the offensive player. Flopping is considered unsportsmanlike. Yet, flopping is practiced by many professional players. In 2008, the NBA decided it would suspend floppers for repeat offenses.

Confessions of an NBA Flopper

I admit it. I am a flopper.

_____
_____
_____
_____
_____
_____
_____
_____
_____
_____
_____
_____

B. You read about the SBA, or the Street Basketball Association. Should streetball be a recognized sport like basketball? Write your opinion as a blog entry. Use examples to show the difference between basketball and streetball.

_____
_____
_____
_____
_____
_____
_____
_____
_____
_____
_____

Name _____ Date _____

Review Vocabulary

A. Read the paragraph. Write a word from the box that BEST completes each sentence.

assembled	symbol	compete	benefit	opposed	expert

Athletes from the five major regions of the world compete in the Olympic Games. When you look at the five rings of the Olympic _____, think of the five regions. Athletes and spectators from hundreds of countries _____ for the summer Olympic Games. My family and I watched the games on TV. First, we saw athletes carry the torch in the traditional relay before the games started. Swimming is my sport. I wanted to see the U.S. swimmers _____ for the gold medal. Only _____ swimmers make it to the Olympics. After the athletes _____ one another, the winners and losers shook hands. Olympic athletes make friendships that _____ them throughout their lives.

B. Complete each sentence by writing a context clue that supports the meaning of the boldfaced word. The first one is done for you.

1. Throughout history, the Olympic Games have undergone a significant **transition**, or
   _____**developmental change**_____.

2. Journalists from **media**, such as _____, reported the results of the Super Bowl.

3. When people choose a sports hero, that player is their idea of the **ideal**, or _____, athlete.

4. If you teach children how to play soccer, what **motion**, or _____, would you make them practice most?

5. Many teens in New York City play basketball in **urban** parks. The parks are located _____.

6. Despite political differences, the countries marched under one flag to demonstrate their **tolerance**, or _____, of one another.

Name _____ Date _____

Extend Vocabulary

A. The word *critics* comes from the Greek root meaning "judge or decide." Read the following words and their meanings. Notice how all the word meanings connect to the words *judge* and *decide*.

critics (n)   *those who express a negative viewpoint after judging*

criteria (n)   *standards or rules used to judge something*

critical (adj)   *expressing disapproving judgments*

criticize (v)   *state judgments of the faults of someone or something*

criticism (n)   *an expression of disapproval based on judgment*

critique (n)   *a detailed analysis and assessment of something*

B. Choose the boldfaced word from Part A that BEST completes each sentence.

1. The newspaper journalists wrote a brief _____ of the athletes' poor sportsmanship.

2. Louis and Andy disagree with _____ who say boxing is too violent.

3. Many fans complain about professional athletes. Mainly, the fans are _____ of the million-dollar salaries.

4. Judges at the Olympics follow a set of _____ to assess the athletes.

5. In his book, the sportswriter gave an informative _____ of the U.S. gymnastic team's performance in the Olympics.

6. Is it good sportsmanship to _____ a teammate's mistake?

C. Write two sentences about sports. Use one boldfaced word from Part A in each sentence.

1. _____

2. _____

Name _____ Date _____

Assess Comprehension and Vocabulary

A. Read the following passage. Look for sequences of events. Remember to make connections between the text, your life, other texts you have read, and the world.

> The Olympic torch is a tradition that began in Ancient Greece. The torch relay went through a transition. It started as a competition and now is a symbol of peace and goodwill. Ancient Greeks used the sun's rays and a mirror to light a flame. It burned constantly in Olympia at the altar for the goddess Hestia. Every four years, during a festival for the goddess Athena, relay teams would compete by passing a flame. Later, the Ancient Olympic Games began. To announce the games, messengers traveled on foot telling everyone that the games would be a time of peace and tolerance. In modern times, the Olympic torch relay is noncompetitive. The sacred flame still is lit in Olympia with a mirror and the sun. Then, runners pass the flame all the way to the Olympics host city. Once spectators and athletes have assembled for the Opening Ceremonies, the last torchbearer uses the flame to light a cauldron at the stadium.

B. Circle the letter of each correct answer.

1. What is NOT a synonym for the word *transition*?
   A. change
   B. development
   C. advantage
   D. transformation

2. Which word does NOT go with *compete*?
   A. oppose
   B. tradition
   C. relay
   D. race

3. What is an antonym for the word *tolerance*?
   A. prejudice
   B. acceptance
   C. respect
   D. goodwill

4. What could be a *symbol*?
   A. flag
   B. sign
   C. logo
   D. all of the above

5. Which definition BEST fits the word *assembled*?
   A. agreed with one another
   B. cooperated together
   C. competed against
   D. gathered together

Name _____   Date _____

6. What is the topic of this passage?

   A. people who have carried the Olympic torch

   B. the history of the torch relay

   C. different types of relay races

   D. Ancient Greek gods and goddesses

7. What would be a good title for this passage?

   A. Training for the Olympics

   B. Fire in Greek Mythology

   C. Carrying the Flame of Peace

   D. The Olympic Opening Ceremonies

8. What is the same about the ancient and modern flames at Olympia?

   A. The flames were lit at the end of a race.

   B. The flames are for the goddess Hestia.

   C. They are lit with the sun's rays and a mirror.

   D. An Olympic athlete lit the flames.

9. Which is the BEST connection to the ancient Greek relay tradition and festival?

   A. Today, we have similar traditions in the World Series.

   B. Today, the Olympic Games torch still is passed through a relay.

   C. Today, the Olympic Games are not competitive.

   D. Today, the Olympic Games honor Greek goddesses.

10. Which statement about fire and flames does NOT connect well to the passage?

   A. Flames remind me of good things like warmth and light.

   B. Flames in campfires and forests can be very dangerous.

   C. I visited a monument with an eternal flame that honors fallen soldiers.

   D. When a candle flame keeps burning, it means hope to me.

11. What is true of both the ancient messengers and modern Olympic torchbearers?

   A. They journey across the globe.

   B. They light a cauldron at a stadium.

   C. They carry and pass on a torch.

   D. They travel after the Olympics.

12. Read these events. Which happens first?

   A. Ancient Greeks light a flame to Hestia in Olympia.

   B. Ancient Greeks hold Olympic Games.

   C. Messengers carry a torch before the ancient games.

   D. Modern runners light a cauldron at the stadium.

Name _____   **Date** _____

13. Which of these events happens last?

    A. The festival for Athena is held every four years.

    B. The Olympic torch relay begins in modern times.

    C. A constant flame burns for the goddess Hestia.

    D. Messengers spread news of peace and the Ancient Olympic Games.

14. What happens after the last torchbearer reaches the Olympics host city?

    A. The torch travels throughout the world.

    B. The sacred flame is lit in Olympia.

    C. The torchbearer lights the cauldron.

    D. Runners pass on the torch.

15. Number the following items in the correct order:

    ____ The torch is lit in Olympia.

    ____ Spectators and athletes assemble for the opening ceremonies.

    ____ Runners carry and pass the torch.

    ____ The torchbearer lights the cauldron at the stadium in the host cities.

Name _____   Date _____

Reteach

A. Read the following passage. Look for sequences of events. Think about how the passage is similar to your life, other texts you have read, and the world.

> Imagine surviving seven days in the desert. Now imagine surviving a 150-mile footrace through the desert. That's the 4 Deserts race. This race occurs over a year through the hottest, coldest, driest, and windiest places on Earth. Actually, it is series of races that begins in the Atacama Desert in Chile and continues through the Gobi Desert in China and the Sahara Desert in Egypt. Finally, competitors finish in Antarctica. Athletes from countries all over the world join to experience this journey of a lifetime. Competitors run or walk and carry their own equipment and food. They are provided with water, tents, and medical assistance. In the evening, they meet to rest and visit around campfires. At each stop, racers can enjoy interesting sights and experiences in their surroundings. When these competitors return home, they have amazing stories to tell about how they tested their minds and bodies to the limit.

B. Answer the questions about the passage.

1. The text states: *Imagine surviving seven days in the desert. Now imagine surviving a 150-mile footrace through the desert.* How does this help you connect your experience to the text?

   _____

   _____

2. The following is an example of a personal connection to the text: *I feel proud of myself whenever I accomplish something challenging.* Focus on key words like *desert*, *footrace*, *to the limit*, or other words that grab your attention. Write a connection to your own life experiences.

   _____

   _____

3. Use what you already know about deserts to make a connection to the text.

   I know that deserts _____

   _____.

Name _____ Date _____

4. Think about these parts of the text: *Gobi Desert in China, the Atacama Desert in Chile, the Sahara Desert in Egypt, and Antarctica"* and *"These are some of the hottest, coldest, driest, and windiest places on Earth."* Complete the following statements.

These deserts remind me of something I read in books or saw in the media. It was _____
_____.

It helps me understand more about the 4 Deserts race because _____
_____.

5. Write your own personal connection to this sentence: *When these competitors return home, they have amazing stories to tell about how they tested their minds and bodies to the limit.*
This reminds me _____
_____.

6. Look back at "The Real Winner Doesn't Always Get the Gold." What connection can you make between that passage and the passage in Part A?

_____

_____

_____

_____

7. Number the following items in the real-time order they would happen in the 4 Deserts race.

_____ They complete traveling across the fourth desert by the end of the year.

_____ They rest and visit around campfires.

_____ At the beginning of the year, competitors start running or walking in one desert.

_____ Participants come home having tested their mental and physical limitations.

8. If you were in the 4 Deserts race, where would you start and end?

Start _____

End _____

Name _____ Date _____

Real World—Box Score

Read the USA box score from the 2008 men's basketball gold medal game against Spain. As you read the box score, answer the following questions.

1. Circle the winning score.
2. Who scored the most points? _____
3. Who spent the most time on the court? _____
4. Which team members did not play at all? _____

Country	Q1	Q2	Q3	Q4	Total
Spain	31	30	21	25	107

Country	Q1	Q2	Q3	Q4	Total
USA	38	31	22	27	118

	USA	Min	FG M/A	FG %	2pts M/A	2pts %	3pts M/A	3pts %	FT M/A	FT %	Rbs O	Rbs D	Tot	As	PF	To	St	BS	Pts
4	C. Boozer	0	0/0	0	0/0	0	0/0	0	0/0	00	0	0	0	0	0	0	0	0	0
5	J. Kidd	11	1/1	100	1/1	100	0/0	0	0/0	0	0	1	1	0	2	0	0	0	2
6	L. James	28	6/9	66.7	4/6	66.7	2/3	66.7	0/2	0	1	5	6	3	4	3	3	1	14
7	D. Williams	16	2/5	40	1/3	33.3	1/2	50	2/2	100	0	1	1	1	3	2	1	0	7
8	M. Redd	0	0/0	0	0/0	0	0/0	0	0/0	0	0	0	0	0	0	0	0	0	0
9	D. Wade	27	9/12	75	5/5	100	4/7	57.1	5/7	71.4	0	2	2	2	3	3	4	0	27
10	K. Bryant	27	7/14	50	4/6	66.7	3/8	37.5	3/3	100	0	3	3	6	4	3	0	0	20
11	D. Howard	17	3/3	100	3/3	100	0/0	0	2/6	33.3	2	3	5	0	4	0	0	0	8
12	C. Bosh	23	1/2	50	1/2	50	0/0	0	6/6	100	2	5	7	0	0	0	0	0	8
13	C. Paul	24	2/5	40	2/4	50	0/1	0	9/10	90	0	3	3	5	3	1	2	0	13
14	T. Prince	8	3/3	100	3/3	100	0/0	0	0/0	0	2	0	2	0	1	0	0	0	6
15	C. Anthony	17	5/11	45.5	2/4	50	3/7	42.9	0/1	0	1	0	1	0	2	1	0	0	13
	TOTALS:	198	39/65	60	26/37	70.3	13/28	46.4	27/37	73	8	23	31	17	26	13	10	3	118

Legend					
Min	Minutes Played	**Tot**	Total Rebounds	**BS**	Block Shots
M/A	Made/Attempts	**As**	Assists	**Pts**	Points
%	Shooting Percentage	**PF**	Personal Fouls	**Rbs**	Rebounds
O	Offensive Rebounds	**To**	Turnovers	**FG**	Field Goal/Basket
D	Defensive Rebounds	**St**	Steals	**FT**	Free Throw

Name _____ Date _____

Exploring Careers: Physical Therapist

A. Answer the following questions about a career as a physical therapist.

1. What are four different places where a physical therapist might work?

   _____

2. What interests, skills, or abilities fit with a career as a physical therapist?

   _____

   _____

3. What education does a physical therapist need?

   _____

   _____

4. What is the average annual salary range for physical therapists in the United States?

   _____

5. How might a job as a physical therapist be rewarding?

   _____

   _____

   _____

B. Use the Internet to research other possible career choices in this field and complete the chart.	
Career	
Responsibilities	
Education Required	
Average Salary	
Is this a career you might pursue?	
Why or why not?	
Career	
Responsibilities	
Education Required	
Average Salary	
Is this a career you might pursue?	
Why or why not?	

Name _____   Date _____

Vocabulary

"Steroids and Health"

A. Rate your knowledge of each boldfaced word.

   3   I know what this word means, and I can use it in a sentence.

   2   I have an idea of this word's meaning, but I need to know more.

   1   I don't know what this word means.

☐   **speculate** (v) *wonder or guess about something without knowing all the facts*
His dramatic increase in muscle has led some to *speculate* that he is using anabolic steroids.

☐   **chemicals** (n) *substances formed when two or more other substances act upon one another*
Scientists can combine substances to make *chemicals* that aid in muscle growth.

☐   **organic** (adj) *made using only natural products*
Organic drugs are made without the use of artificial chemicals.

☐   **synthesized** (v) *produced a substance by a chemical or biological process*
Scientists are able to artificially create many hormones that are *synthesized* by the body.

☐   **soluble** (adj) *can be dissolved in liquid*
Many chemicals are water *soluble*, making them undetectable to the drinker.

☐   **effects** (n) *the results or consequences of something*
An increase in body hair is one of the *effects* of anabolic steroid use.

B. Choose the boldfaced vocabulary word from Part A that BEST answers each question.

1. Which word goes with saying what you may do five years from now? _____

2. Which word goes with why it's easy to stir sugar into hot tea? _____

3. Which word goes with "an athlete's performance after sports training"? _____

4. Which word goes with sodium and fat that act upon each other in ordinary soap? _____

5. Which word goes with "natural"? _____

6. Which word goes with "produced in a laboratory"? _____

Name _____   Date _____

Ask Questions

Before reading "Steroids and Health," ask questions about the headings. During reading, answer each question and ask another question. Answer the new questions after reading.

Before Reading	During Reading	After Reading
Question: Do all top athletes use drugs to win?	**Answer:** Some top athletes may be accused of using drugs because their performance makes it seem that way.	
	New Question: Has it ever been proven that Lance Armstrong used banned drugs to win?	**Answer:**
Question:	**Answer:**	
	New Question:	**Answer:**
Question:	**Answer:**	
	New Question:	**Answer:**
Question:	**Answer:**	
	New Question:	**Answer:**
Question:	**Answer:**	
	New Question:	**Answer:**

Name _____   Date _____

Word Building

A. In English, *ch* has the /ch/ sound in words like *chip* or *chart*. In Greek, *ch* has the /k/ sound as in *chemical*. The following list has other words with Greek origins. Read the words and their meanings.

archaic (adj)	*outdated; no longer in ordinary use*
chaos (n)	*state of disorder and confusion*
character (n)	*the way a person thinks, feels, and acts; personality*
chasm (n)	*wide difference between ideas or feelings*
lichen (n)	*algae-like organism that grows on trees*
melancholy (adj)	*sad*
orchid (n)	*flowering plant usually found in the tropics*
psychology (n)	*study of human and animal behavior*
schooner (n)	*ship or sailing vessel with two masts and sails set lengthwise*

B. Choose the BEST word from Part A to complete each sentence. Look for a context clue that helps you understand the meaning. The first one is done for you.

1. When the fans heard an explosion in the soccer stadium, the ordinary game turned into a state of confusion, or _____**chaos**_____.

2. Some groups want random drug testing for high school athletes, and other groups are against it. A great difference of ideas, or _____, exists between these groups.

3. Some people feel that using urine tests to detect illegal drug use is outdated, or _____.

4. An athlete who is disqualified because of steroid use might be sad, or _____, in later years.

5. Some fans choose a sports hero for her excellent ability when playing the sport and for her fine _____, or the way she thinks and acts throughout her life.

C. Write two sentences about a challenge you face. Use one or more of the boldfaced words from Part A in each sentence.

1. _____

2. _____

Name _____   Date _____

Write in Response to Reading

LaMarr is a high school football player. A couple of his friends have used steroids. They have tried to convince LaMarr to use steroids too. LaMarr has been told that he will become stronger if he uses the substance. LaMarr would rather work hard over the summer and do it on his own, but sometimes he is unsure. One night he has a vivid dream. He dreams many people are giving him advice. In the graphic organizer are the people in LaMarr's dream. Write what they say and what LaMarr decides to do when he wakes up.

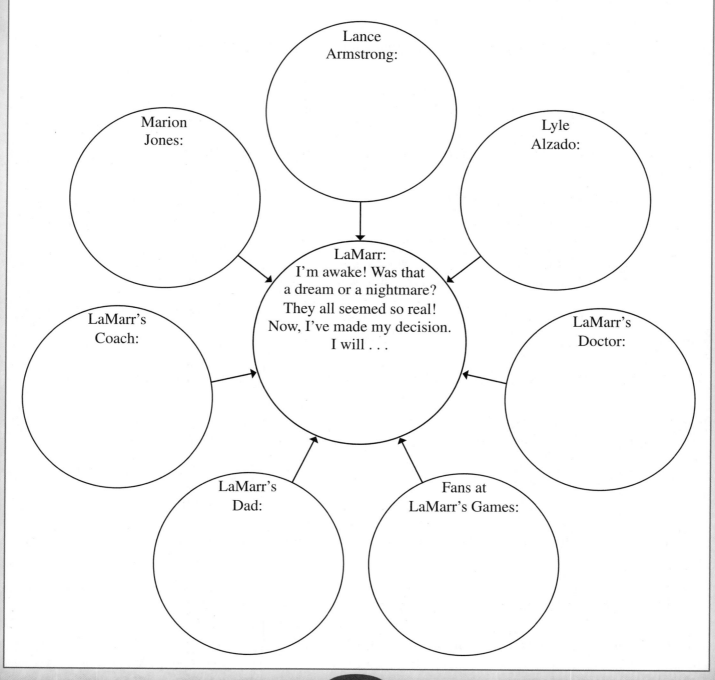

Name _____ Date _____

Vocabulary

"Mixed Martial Arts: Sport and Media Show"

A. Write one or more numbers next to each boldfaced word to show when you have seen, heard, or used this word.

5   I use it in everyday conversation.
4   I heard it on TV or on the radio.
3   I heard or used it in school.
2   I read it in a book, magazine, or online.
1   I have not read, heard, or used this word.

☐   **competent** (adj) *having the skill or ability to do something well*
Competent fighters have what it takes to win.

☐   **endeavors** (v) *tries very hard to do something*
Each fighter *endeavors* to knock out the other fighter.

☐   **maneuvers** (n) *difficult movements that require planning and skill*
Fighters use difficult *maneuvers* to force the other fighter to tap out, or quit.

☐   **vary** (v) *be different*
The moves used in martial arts *vary* from discipline to discipline.

☐   **adhere** (v) *stick with an idea, plan, or rules*
If opponents do not *adhere* to the rules, someone could be injured seriously.

☐   **spectacle** (n) *a remarkable and dramatic sight*
The first Ultimate Fighting Championship was a *spectacle* watched by many people.

B. Read the following questions, then answer each one.

1. Would you use **maneuvers** to describe the movements of professional wrestlers or of children playing tag? _____

2. If you wanted to **vary** your skills at sports, would you focus on one sport or try different sports? _____

3. If Max said he saw a **spectacle**, did he see something ordinary or unusual? _____

4. If athletes **adhere** to a training and practice schedule, will they miss many sessions or attend every session? _____

5. Would a coach expect a **competent** athlete to play well or play poorly? _____

6. Would a person who **endeavors** to win try hard or quit? _____

Name _____ Date _____

Word Building

A. The *eu* spelling pattern usually makes the /ü/ sound, like in *maneuvers*. In some cases, it makes the /yü/ sound. Read other words, pronunciations, and definitions with the same spelling pattern in the box.

/ü/

neurons (n)   *nerve cells*

neutral (adj)   *revealing no attitude or feeling*

pneumatic (adj)   *using compressed air to create greater power*

sleuth (n)   *an investigator*

/yü/

therapeutic (adj)   *used to cure, restore, or maintain health*

eulogy (n)   *spoken or written tribute to someone who has died*

feud (n)   *a long-term disagreement or dispute*

queue (n)   *a line of a people or objects*

B. Choose the BEST word from Part A to complete each statement.

1. Fans looked forward to an exciting fight. The competitors had not spoken to each other since last year's fight. They were having a _____.

2. The mixed martial arts fighter had injuries to _____ and other brain cells.

3. Referees are trained to be completely fair and _____.

4. When someone dies, a family member usually delivers the _____.

5. A sportswriter reported that the fighter pounded his fists like a _____ drill.

6. People will wait in a long _____ to buy tickets for MMA matches.

7. Before a match, a boxing trainer is like a _____ because he discovers the strengths and weaknesses of the competitor.

8. Some competitors believe hot tubs are _____.

C. Choose two words from Part A. Write a sentence for each word.

1. _____

2. _____

Name _____   Date _____

Cause and Effect

Read the following instances of cause and effect from "Mixed Martial Arts: Sport and Media Show." Write each in the correct order in the cause-and-effect chain diagram. The first one is done for you.

- Mixed martial arts (MMA) begins as a full-contact, no rules sport.
- The organization creates new rules, sponsors, and publicity.
- MMA becomes an accepted sport.
- People criticize the Ultimate Fighting Championship (UFC) for promoting violence.
- Competitors are unmatched because they are not in weight classes.
- The combat is unfair.

Cause-and-Effect Chain

Cause: Mixed martial arts (MMA) begins as a full-contact, no rules sport.

↓

Effect/Cause:

↓

Effect/Cause:

↓

Effect/Cause:

↓

Effect/Cause:

↓

Effect:

Name _____ Date _____

Write in Response to Reading

A. Create a job profile for a mixed martial arts competitor. Include the requirements, duties, location, hours, pay, and hazards of the job.

> **Profile: Mixed Martial Arts Competitor**
>
> **Candidate Requirements:**
>
>
> **Job Duties:**
>
> **Location:**
>
> **Hours:**
>
> **Compensation:**
>
> **Possible Highlights of the Job:**
>
> **Possible Hazards:**

B. Create a poem, rap, or song lyrics with a title about a mixed martial arts fighter from one of the following viewpoints.
- a close family member
- an adoring fan
- the greatest rival of the fighter

> **Title:**

Name _____   Date _____

Review Vocabulary

A. Complete each sentence by writing a context clue that supports the meaning of the boldfaced word.

1. When you watch professional sports, you will notice that some game rules **vary**, or _____, from amateur sports.

2. The powder for the energy drink is **soluble** so it can _____.

3. Steroids are **chemicals**, or _____, that aid in muscle growth.

4. Testosterone is an **organic** hormone. It exists _____ the human body.

5. Defensive **maneuvers**, or _____, are part of martial arts.

6. Scientists **synthesized**, or _____, molecules in the lab.

B. Read the following interview. Write a word from the box that BEST completes each sentence.

effects	speculate	competent	endeavors
adhere	spectacle	evokes	banned

Olympic gold medalist Tamara describes winning a gold medal and forfeiting it because of steroids. She tells her story to news correspondent Dennis.

Dennis: Thanks for joining me today, Tamara. Your record-breaking 1600-meter run was quite a _____! Tell us about that experience.

Tamara: First off, thanks for inviting me to tell my story. Every Olympic athlete _____ to win the gold. For me, the experience was phenomenal. However, the memory also _____ regret.

Dennis: Many people began to _____ that you'd used steroids when your performance dramatically improved.

Tamara: Yes, the Olympic committee had _____ the use of steroids. I did not _____ to those rules. That's my reason for regret and for giving up my medal. The _____ of steroids on my strength and endurance were extraordinary. I felt more and more _____ as I practiced. I knew I would be a winner. But, in the end, my victory was a fake.

Name _____   Date _____

Extend Vocabulary

A. The words *speculate* and *spectacle* contain the Latin root *specere*, meaning "watch or look." Read the following words and their meanings. Notice how all the word meanings connect to the words *watch* and *look*.

aspects (n)	*specific parts or features of someone or something you've seen*
spectacle (n)	*a remarkable and dramatic sight*
spectators (n)	*people who watch at an event, such as a show or game*
inspect (v)	*looked at closely to assess the condition of a person or thing*
speculate (v)	*wonder or guess about something you've seen without knowing all the facts*
introspective (adj)	*reflective; looking at one's own thoughts and feelings*

B. Think about the meanings of the words in Part A and how you have heard each word used. Choose the word from Part A that BEST completes each sentence.

1. The Olympic stadium was filled with _____ from all over the world.

2. When fans enter a stadium, guards _____ all of the bags they are carrying.

3. Martial arts movements blend _____ of grace and fierceness.

4. The bodybuilder's sudden increase in strength led everyone to _____ that he used steroids.

5. After she lost the track race, Myra was quiet and _____, thinking about what she had done wrong.

6. Olympic figure skating is a _____ watched by viewers across the world.

C. Write two sentences about a sports event. Use a boldfaced word from Part A in each sentence.

1. _____

2. _____

Name _____ Date _____

Assess Comprehension and Vocabulary

A. Read the following passage. Look for a cause-and-effect chain.

> You may think that extremely violent sports are unique to modern American culture. However, the thrill of blood and possible death during fighting matches entertained the Romans thousands of years ago. Gladiator combat was a common lethal spectacle during the Roman Empire. Gladiators were slaves, criminals, or professional fighters. The opponents would vary from fight to fight. Gladiators fought other gladiators, wild animals, and condemned criminals. Some matches were fought to the death. Imagine a crowd of spectators. The audience requests specific gladiators. Two armored men meet in the center of the arena. Each endeavors to kill his opponent. They fight until one raises his finger, a signal of defeat. A referee steps in to stop the fight. A decision is made based on what most pleases the crowd. The crowd might signal for the loser to be killed. According to gladiator bones, we can speculate that a winning opponent would thrust his sword downward into the neck and pierce the heart. Several emperors attempted to ban gladiator combats because of the violence. However, Romans did not adhere to the bans for several decades.

B. Circle the letter of each correct answer.

1. Which word does NOT describe a *spectacle*?
   A. remarkable
   B. common
   C. dramatic
   D. impressive

2. Which word is a synonym for *vary*?
   A. isolate
   B. compare
   C. contend
   D. differ

3. Which word is NOT a synonym for *endeavors*?
   A. tries
   B. attempts
   C. plays
   D. strives

4. Which word is a synonym for *speculate*?
   A. plan
   B. wonder
   C. observe
   D. start

Name _____   Date _____

5. Which word is an antonym for *adhere*?

   A. ignore

   B. obey

   C. agree

   D. follow

6. What is the topic of this passage?

   A. entertainment in Rome

   B. gladiator combat

   C. the history of boxing

   D. Roman criminals

7. What would be a good title for this passage?

   A. Gladiator Combat: a Violent Spectacle

   B. Slaves and Criminals on Trial

   C. Violence in American Culture

   D. Weak Emperors and Bans on Roman Combat

8. Spectators went to gladiator combat for the purpose of . . .

   A. enjoying entertainment.

   B. choosing the gladiators.

   C. seeing an exciting combat spectacle.

   D. all of the above.

9. A gladiator might raise his finger and give up the fight. What would cause the winner to kill the loser?

   A. The winner wanted to prove he was fearless.

   B. The spectators signaled for the loser to die.

   C. The winner was afraid the loser was faking and might attack.

   D. The spectators signaled that the fight was too violent.

10. What caused the referee to stop the fight?

   A. A gladiator broke a rule.

   B. The emperor issued a ban.

   C. The audience signaled a stop.

   D. A gladiator signaled defeat.

11. What caused the emperors to ban gladiator combat?

   A. The arenas became too crowded.

   B. The fights were too violent.

   C. There were no surviving gladiators.

   D. Roman spectators got bored.

12. What was NOT a possible effect of the gladiator's finger signal?

   A. The referee halted the combat.

   B. The crowd made a decision.

   C. The emperor interrupted the gladiators.

   D. The defeated gladiator was killed.

Name _____ Date _____

13. Why would gladiators have different opponents including other gladiators, wild animals, and criminals?

   A. Romans needed a way to get rid of wild animals.

   B. Jails for criminals were not common during the Roman Empire.

   C. It was more entertaining to have different types of fighters.

   D. It was too difficult to find competent gladiators.

14. What did NOT lead up to the gladiator's signal?

   A. The crowd signaled the loser's death.

   B. The crowd selected gladiators.

   C. Each man endeavored to kill the other.

   D. The gladiator realized he was defeated.

15. Read the first sentence marked 1. Number the other sentences in cause-and-effect order.

   _1_ **The crowd selects gladiators.**

   ___ Each gladiator endeavors to kill the other.

   ___ The crowd signals the loser's death.

   ___ The victorious gladiator kills the loser.

   ___ Two armored men meet in the arena's center.

   ___ The referee interrupts the combat.

   ___ A gladiator signals defeat.

Name _____   **Date** _____

Reteach

A. Read the following passage. Look for a cause-and-effect chain.

> A triple play is one of the most exciting and rare plays in baseball. In a triple play, three consecutive outs occur in a single play. Here is one way it can happen. Runners are on first and second base. The batter comes to the plate and hits the ball. The shortstop picks up the ground ball and throws it to the third baseman. The third baseman then steps on the base, and the runner coming from second is out. The third baseman throws the ball to the second baseman who tags out the runner coming from first base. Finally, the second baseman throws the ball to first base. The first baseman steps on first base, and the batter is out. It's a triple play! The inning is over.

B. Complete the cause-and-effect chain about a triple play.

The batter hits the ball to the shortstop.

↓

The shortstop

↓

The third baseman

↓

The third baseman

↓

The second baseman

↓

The second baseman

↓

The first baseman

↓

Three outs—the inning is

Name _____   Date _____

C. Imagine the shortstop missed the ball. Create a new cause-and-effect chain.

```
┌──────────────────────────────────────────────────────────────┐
│                                                                │
└──────────────────────────────────────────────────────────────┘
                               │
                               ▼
┌──────────────────────────────────────────────────────────────┐
│                                                                │
└──────────────────────────────────────────────────────────────┘
                               │
                               ▼
┌──────────────────────────────────────────────────────────────┐
│                                                                │
└──────────────────────────────────────────────────────────────┘
                               │
                               ▼
┌──────────────────────────────────────────────────────────────┐
│                                                                │
└──────────────────────────────────────────────────────────────┘
                               │
                               ▼
┌──────────────────────────────────────────────────────────────┐
│                                                                │
└──────────────────────────────────────────────────────────────┘
                               │
                               ▼
┌──────────────────────────────────────────────────────────────┐
│                                                                │
└──────────────────────────────────────────────────────────────┘
                               │
                               ▼
┌──────────────────────────────────────────────────────────────┐
│                                                                │
└──────────────────────────────────────────────────────────────┘
                               │
                               ▼
┌──────────────────────────────────────────────────────────────┐
│                                                                │
└──────────────────────────────────────────────────────────────┘
```

Name _____ Date _____

Real World—Training Program

Read the following training schedule.

4-Week Training Program for Runners

Important Reminder: You should always consult a doctor before you begin a new program of exercise.

Weeks 1 and 2—
Monday, Wednesday, Saturday*
Total Time: 38 minutes

 Warm-Up Exercises and Stretches
When: Before each workout
What: Gentle warm-up exercises and
stretches**
Duration: 5 minutes

 Warm-Up Walk
When: Before each workout
What: Walk at a moderate pace
Duration: 5 minutes

 Main Running Pattern
When: After warm-up exercises and walk
What: Alternate jogging for 1 minute
and walking for 5 minutes
Duration: 24 minutes

 Cool-Down Exercises and Stretches
When: After each workout
What: Gentle cool-down exercises and
stretches**
Duration: 4 minutes

Weeks 3 and 4—
Tuesday, Thursday, Sunday*
Total Time: 40 minutes

 Warm-Up Exercises and Stretches
When: Before each workout
What: Gentle warm-up exercises and
stretches**
Duration: 5 minutes

 Warm-Up Walk
When: Before each workout
What: Walk at a brisk pace
Duration: 5 minutes

 Main Running Pattern
When: After warm-up exercises and walk
What: Alternate jogging 1.5 minutes
and walking for 5 minutes
Duration: 26 minutes

 Cool-Down Exercises and Stretches
When: After each workouts
What: Gentle cool-down exercises and
stretches**
Duration: 4 minutes

*You can alter the days, but you should keep them spread out throughout the week.
**These exercises and stretches work well for either warming up or cooling down. Refer to our guide
for instructions for these and other exercises/stretches.

- Wall push-ups
- Hamstring stretches
- Groin stretches
- Back stretches
- Heel to buttock stretches
- Lower back and hip stretches

Name _____   Date _____

Answer the questions about the training program.

1. Who is the training for? _____

2. How long is the total workout time in Weeks 1 and 2? _____

3. What do you always do after you run? _____

4. How do you warm up? _____

5. What does * mean? _____

   _____

6. How long is the total workout time in Weeks 3 and 4? _____

7. In the main running pattern, what do you alternate with jogging? _____

8. Do you spend more time walking or jogging in the program? _____

9. Why would it be important to consult a physician before beginning an exercise program?

   _____

10. Would this training program would be easy to follow? Explain. _____

   _____

Name _____ Date _____

Exploring Careers: Athletic Trainer/Coach

A. Answer the following questions about a career as an athletic trainer or athletic coach.

1. What are three important tasks that an athletic trainer does on the job?

   _____

2. What education does an athletic trainer need?

   _____

   _____

3. What is the average annual salary range for an athletic trainer who works for a company?

   _____

4. What are three responsibilities of an athletic coach?

   _____

   _____

5. What knowledge and interests would fit with a career as an athletic trainer or coach?

   _____

   _____

   _____

B. Use the Internet to research other possible career choices in this field and complete the chart.

Career	
Responsibilities	
Education Required	
Average Salary	
Is this a career you might pursue?	
Why or why not?	
Career	
Responsibilities	
Education Required	
Average Salary	
Is this a career you might pursue?	
Why or why not?	

Name _____   Date _____

A. Organize Your Ideas

Giving Your All

-
-
-

How can you overcome obstacles that could make it difficult to obtain your goals?	Who in your life would help you overcome a great difficulty? Why did you choose that person?	Why do some people in emergency situations have great strength or courage?
• • •	• • •	• • •

What else would you like to know about overcoming obstacles?

_____

_____

B. The Big Picture

In Expedition 14, you will discover how people deal with and overcome great challenges and difficulties in life. Write the big idea of each passage in the outside boxes. Connect the passages in the center box by writing the big picture.

"Fight or Flight"
helped me understand . . .

"Team Hoyt," "Liz Murray," "Josh Hamilton"
After reading about these people, I learned . . .

Big Picture
When I think about what people face in life, I can see that . . .

"Aron Ralston: Trapped in the Canyon," and "Bethany Hamilton: Riding the Waves"
helped me realize . . .

"9/11: Terror from the Sky" and "Flight 93"
made me wonder . . .

C. Expedition Dictionary

You will read the following vocabulary words throughout the Expedition. As you learn the words, use them as often as possible in your oral and written language.

"Fight or Flight"

situation	(n) *condition or state of affairs*
instances	(n) *occurrences or things that happen*
affect	(v) *bring about a change*

"Team Hoyt"

inspiring	(adj) *stimulating or exalting to the spirit*
achieve	(v) *succeed in doing; accomplish*
disabilities	(n) *physical or mental handicaps*

"Liz Murray"

background	(n) *a person's training and experience*
poverty	(n) *condition of being poor; lack of money*
academic	(adj) *having to do with schools, colleges, or teaching*

"Josh Hamilton"

nominated	(v) *named as a candidate for election*
enforced	(v) *made to obey*
blunders	(n) *ideas, answers, or acts that are wrong; mistakes*

"Aron Ralston: Trapped in the Canyon"

solitude	(n) *being alone*
disastrous	(adj) *causing great distress or injury*
desperate	(adj) *very serious with little or no hope*

"Bethany Hamilton: Riding the Waves"

severed	(v) *cut off or apart*
ferocious	(adj) *fierce; savage*
impair	(v) *weaken or damage*

"9/11: Terror from the Sky"

collapsed	(v) *fell down suddenly*
heroic	(adj) *showing great bravery or daring like a hero*
gratitude	(n) *feeling of being grateful for something; appreciation*

"Flight 93"

anguish	(n) *great suffering caused by worry, grief, or pain; agony*
valor	(n) *courage or bravery*
confrontation	(n) *an open conflict or clashing of forces*

Dictionary Challenge

Write a description of when you or someone you know overcame an obstacle to achieve a goal or did something heroic. Use as many vocabulary words as possible.

Name _____ Date _____

Vocabulary

"Fight or Flight"

A. Rate your knowledge of each boldfaced vocabulary word.

3 familiar
2 somewhat familiar
1 unknown

situation (n) *condition or state of affairs*
The *situation* changed when the dark figure in the alley turned out to be my neighbor's dog.

instances (n) *occurrences or things that happen*
There have been many *instances* when people have had unusual strength during emergencies.

affect (v) *bring about a change*
Scary movies don't *affect* Jamaal, but they give his little sister nightmares.

B. Circle the word from Part A that BEST completes each sentence.

1. At first, Kim felt awkward when she wore the brace, but now it doesn't (situation, affect) her movements.

2. A speeding car in a crowded shopping area is a dangerous (situation, instances).

3. The customer complained to the manager of the store after three (instances, affect) of receiving the wrong change.

C. The words *affect* and *effect* have different meanings. Most of the time, *affect* is a verb that means "bring about a change." *Effect* is usually a noun meaning "a result" or "what happened." Write *affect* or *effect* to complete each statement.

Hurricanes _____ people, schools, and businesses. One result is a lack of electric power. Another _____ is ruined homes. A lack of clean water can be another negative _____ in a community. How else could a hurricane _____ a community?

Name _____   Date _____

Main Idea and Details

Think about what you read in "Fight or Flight." Complete the diagram to determine the main idea.

1. Write the topic of the passage. Remember that the topic . . .
   - is the general subject.
   - is about the whole passage, not just one part.
   - is not a complete sentence.

Topic:

2. Write the main idea of "Fight or Flight" and details that support it. Remember, the main idea . . .
   - answers the question, *What is the main thing this passage tells you about the topic?*
   - is supported by details in the passage.
   - is a complete sentence.

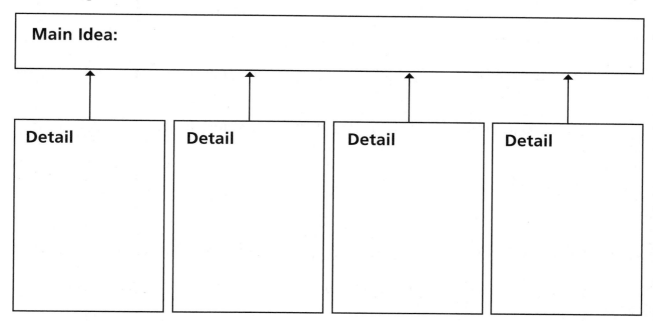

Name _____   Date _____

Vocabulary

"Team Hoyt"

A. Rate your knowledge of each boldfaced word.

3   I know what this word means, and I can use it in a sentence.
2   I have an idea of this word's meaning, but I need to know more.
1   I don't know what this word means.

☐   **inspiring** (adj) *stimulating or exalting to the spirit*
      This *inspiring* message makes me want to be more helpful to people.

☐   **achieve** (v) *succeed in doing; accomplish*
      He will *achieve* his goal by practicing hard every day.

☐   **disabilities** (n) *physical or mental handicaps*
      His *disabilities* did not keep him from competing.

B. Complete each sentence with the correct vocabulary word from Part A.

1. The speaker told an _____ story about how a total stranger saved him from his burning home.

2. Sonia uses computers with special keyboards because she has physical _____.

3. Cade wrote down the athletic goals he plans to _____ during his high school years.

C. Write the vocabulary word from Part A that is the antonym of the underlined word or phrase.

1. Our coach teaches us that practice and teamwork are the way to <u>not reach</u> a victory.

      _____

2. The students' speeches were so <u>disappointing</u> that the audience stood up and cheered.

      _____

3. Some buses have a lift or ramp so that passengers with <u>physical advantages</u> can get on easily.

      _____

Name _____   Date _____

Cause and Effect

Complete each chart by using information from "Team Hoyt" and what you already know.

Cause
Engineers developed a computer for Rick.

↓

Effect

→

Effect

→

Effect

Cause

→

Cause

→

Cause

↓

Effect
Spectators changed from discouraging Team Hoyt to cheering for them to complete races.

Name _____   Date _____

Vocabulary

"Liz Murray"

A. Put a check mark in each row to indicate how well you know each boldfaced word.

	Know This Word	Have Seen This Word	Don't Know This Word
background (n) *a person's training and experience* Liz's difficult *background* did not keep her from reaching her goal.			
poverty (n) *condition of being poor; lack of money* Because of her *poverty*, Liz didn't know how she could pay for college.			
academic (adj) *having to do with schools, colleges, or teaching* Many colleges give *academic* scholarships for students with good grades.			

B. Complete each sentence with the correct vocabulary word from Part A.

1. Jen is working toward a(n) _____ career in teaching or research.

2. Living in a large city and working in a grocery store were part of Hannah's _____.

3. Many cities have programs to help people who are living in _____.

C. The following words and phrases connect to the three vocabulary words in the chart. Decide where each word or phrase BEST belongs and write it in the chart. Use each word or phrase only once.

little money   poor   doing research on the environment   school subjects
five years on a farm   hunger   practicing holiday traditions   taking care of a dog
impoverished   biology   speaking Spanish as a child   professor

poverty	background	academic

Name _____   **Date** _____

Cause and Effect

Complete each chart by using information from "Liz Murray" and what you already know.

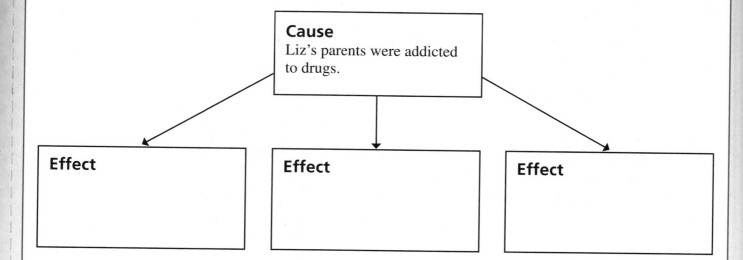

Cause
Liz's parents were addicted to drugs.

Effect

Effect

Effect

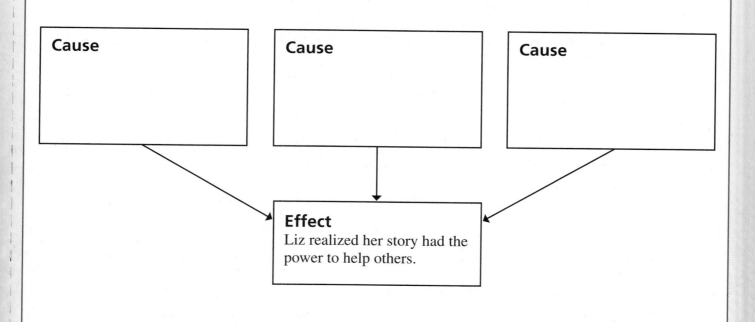

Cause

Cause

Cause

Effect
Liz realized her story had the power to help others.

Name _____   Date _____

Vocabulary

"Josh Hamilton"

A. Rate your knowledge of each boldfaced word.

   3   I know what this word means, and I can use it in a sentence.

   2   I have an idea of this word's meaning, but I need to know more.

   1   I don't know what this word means.

> **nominated** (v) *named as a candidate for election*
> Josh felt proud when the baseball league *nominated* him for an award.

> **enforced** (v) *made to obey*
> The baseball organization *enforced* the rule against drugs so Josh could not play.

> **blunders** (n) *ideas, answers, or acts that are wrong; mistakes*
> Josh knew he was responsible for his *blunders* and did not blame anyone.

B. Choose the vocabulary word from Part A that BEST completes each sentence.

1. After a group of students _____ Ralph for class president, he gave a speech telling what he planned to do to improve the school.

2. Tyrese made many mistakes, but he finally decided to admit his _____ and try to improve.

3. Once the "no texting" policy was posted, teachers _____ the rule in class.

C. For each underlined word, write a synonym from the words in Part A.

1. When Liz made choices, she didn't repeat the <u>mistakes</u> her parents had made.

   _____

2. After the boy called 911 and saved his family from a fire, the town <u>recommended</u> him for an award.

   _____

3. The dean of the school didn't ignore the rules; instead, she <u>carried out</u> every rule.

   _____

Name _____ **Date** _____

Compare and Contrast

Use the three-circle Venn diagram to compare and contrast elements in the passages about Team Hoyt, Liz Murray, and Josh Hamilton.

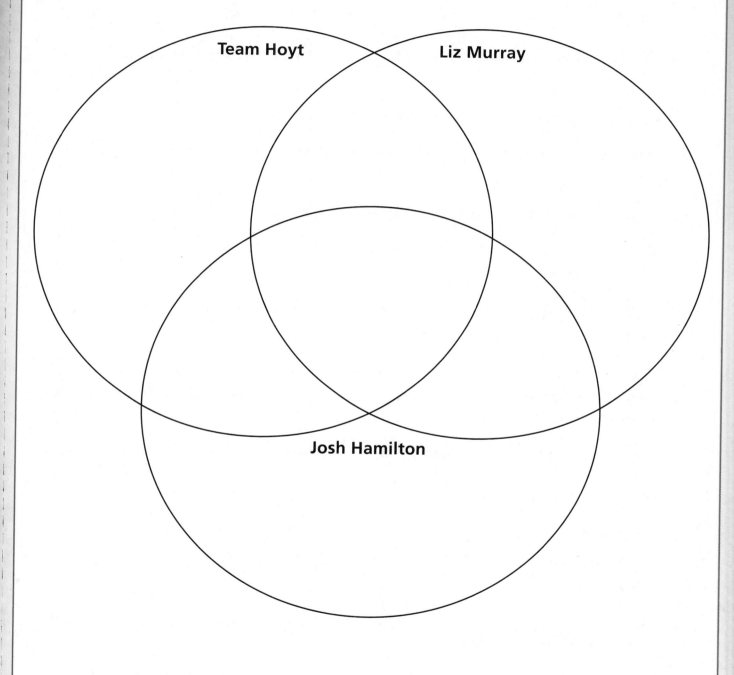

Name _____   Date _____

Review Vocabulary

A. Read the sentences. Choose a word from the box that means the same as each underlined word.

situation	instances	affect	inspiring	background	academic

1. After high school, Anthony worked at a full-time job and went to college part time because it was better for his financial <u>state</u>. _____

2. Emanuel's <u>educational</u> goals include earning his high school diploma. _____

3. Liz Murray understood the obstacles homeless people face because she had a similar <u>experience</u>. _____

4. Liz's story is <u>encouraging</u> to Adrian, who hopes to go to college. _____

5. After his knee operation, Jared did his exercises daily so the injury would not <u>impact</u> his performance on the track team. _____

6. People avoid walking by the vacant lot at night because the newspapers reported <u>occasions</u> of robberies there. _____

B. Complete each sentence by writing the vocabulary word from the box that supports the meaning of the underlined context clue. The first one is done for you.

poverty	enforced	disabilities	achieve	nominated	blunders

1. Julie's parent have experienced _____ poverty _____, but now they have <u>a good income</u>.

2. Faith hopes to _____, or <u>accomplish</u>, her career goals after graduation.

3. He did not let his _____, or <u>physical challenges</u>, stop him from having outdoor adventures.

4. Josh was _____ for an award. The baseball league <u>named him</u> as one of the players who would be honored.

5. Ira was embarrassed about the _____ he made during his speech. He usually doesn't make <u>mistakes</u>.

6. The coaches _____ the school policy against drugs, alcohol, and tobacco. They didn't just <u>ignore</u> the rules.

Name _____ Date _____

Extend Vocabulary

A. Knowing the definition of one word can help you understand the definition of other words. Use your affixionary or dictionary to help you complete the following chart.

achieve	*succeed in doing; accomplish*
achiever	
achievement	
inspiring	*stimulating or exalting to the spirit*
inspiration	
inspired	
inspire	
academic	*having to do with schools, colleges, or teaching*
academically	
academy	

B. Choose a word from Part A to complete each sentence in the paragraph.

Ester went to study law enforcement at the police _____. On graduation day, Ester's family was proud of her _____. Ester's success _____ her younger brother David to study forensics. David had always done well in his high school classes, so he was confident he'd succeed _____ in college. Ester was also an _____ to Tony, her 9-year-old brother. He planned to _____ the position of police detective someday.

Name _____   Date _____

Assess Comprehension and Vocabulary

A. Read the following passage. Remember to notice causes and their effects in the text. Look for similarities and differences between this passage and other passages you have read.

> Benjamin Zephaniah is a poet who was born and raised in Birmingham, England. From a young age, he wrote poetry. When Zephaniah was 10, he started reciting his poetry at his local church. But his academic achievement was poor, and he struggled to learn to read. In his late teens, he found out he had dyslexia, a learning disability that causes reading problems. As a youth, he belonged to street gangs. He was arrested for theft and served a prison sentence. While in prison he decided to improve his reading and writing skills.
>
> Influenced by his Jamaican background, he now writes poetry and performs with Jamaican bands. But Zephaniah wants to achieve more. Through his poetry, novels, plays, and music, he speaks out against racism, war, and animal cruelty. Thirteen universities have nominated him for honorary degrees. Benjamin Zephaniah is inspiring to young readers and writers who believe that they too have important messages to share.

B. Circle the letter of each correct answer.

1. Which definition BEST fits the word *academic*?
   A. bring about change
   B. stimulating or exalting to the spirit
   C. having to do with schools, colleges, or teaching
   D. succeed in doing; accomplish

2. Which word does NOT fit with *background* in the passage?
   A. message
   B. experience
   C. culture
   D. upbringing

3. Which word is a synonym for *achieve*?
   A. compete
   B. accomplish
   C. motivate
   D. take charge of

4. Which word does NOT go with *nominated*?
   A. candidate
   B. chose
   C. named
   D. encouraged

Name _____   Date _____

5. Which definition BEST fits the word
    inspiring?

    A. succeeding in doing; accomplishing

    B. stimulating or exalting to the spirit

    C. occurring or happening

    D. condition or state of affairs

6. What is the topic of this passage?

    A. the life of Benjamin Zephaniah

    B. how Benjamin Zephaniah writes poetry

    C. Benjamin Zephaniah's background
       in Jamaica

    D. how Benjamin Zephaniah learned to read
       and write

7. Which of the following would be a good title
    for this passage?

    A. You Can Become a Poet

    B. A Poet Who Overcame Obstacles

    C. The Rhythms of Jamaican Music

    D. Poetry with a Political Message

8. Which of the following is an effect of
    dyslexia?

    A. It makes it hard to listen to teachers.

    B. Reading is very difficult.

    C. It's hard to memorize poetry.

    D. A person can only read short poetry.

9. Why was Zephaniah arrested?

    A. He stole something.

    B. He was playing loud music.

    C. He was caught doing graffiti.

    D. He was in a political protest.

10. What happened after Zephaniah found out
    that he had dyslexia?

    A. He decided to improve his reading and
       writing skills in prison.

    B. He was expelled from school.

    C. He excelled in science.

    D. He quit reading.

11. According to the passage, why does
    Zephaniah compose poetry?

    A. He wants to prove he can write well.

    B. Poetry is more entertaining for an
       audience.

    C. It's easier than writing stories because
       he has dyslexia.

    D. He wants to educate people about racism,
       war, and animal cruelty.

12. Benjamin Zephaniah and Liz Murray both
    overcame obstacles. What would both say is
    the MOST important way to overcome an
    obstacle in life?

    A. Win a scholarship to study at a college.

    B. Learn to read and write poetry, novels,
       and plays.

    C. Live on the streets when you are young.

    D. Be motivated to overcome the obstacle.

Name _____   Date _____

13. Which statement is true of BOTH Benjamin Zephaniah and Josh Hamilton?

   A. Their main obstacle was substance abuse and addictions.

   B. They speak about their beliefs and try to inspire others.

   C. They won awards in high school.

   D. Their main obstacles were schoolwork and dyslexia.

14. Which difference between Benjamin Zephaniah and Liz Murray is NOT true?

   A. Murray had a physical disability, but Zephaniah had a learning disability.

   B. Murray earned a university degree, but Zephaniah didn't go to college.

   C. Murray had academic talent, but Zephaniah had a talent for writing poetry.

   D. Murray lived in the United States, but Zephaniah lived in England.

15. Summarize the similarities and differences between Benjamin Zephaniah and Liz Murray.

   _____

   _____

   _____

   _____

   _____

   _____

   _____

   _____

   _____

   _____

   _____

   _____

Name _____   Date _____

Reteach

A. Read the following passage.

> He could be hanging upside down from the end of a bungee cord, behind the wheel of a racing boat, or jumping out of a plane. From his daring physical activities, you might never guess that Mike McKeller is disabled. He has a muscle and bone condition that confines him to a wheelchair. Since he was a young boy, he refused to accept his limitations, and he followed his playmates at their every turn. His thirst for adventure sometimes resulted in broken bones. Though his parents tried to set safety guidelines, Mike refused to let his disabilities get in the way of his dreams. He says that his parents "taught me, ingrained in me, that if you really want to do something, figure out how to do it and do it." He has challenged himself in scuba diving, shark fishing, and sky diving. McKeller is a motivational speaker who has been an inspiration to many audiences. He encourages people to think outside their limits and achieve things beyond their wildest dreams.

B. Read the questions about the passage in Part A. Complete each statement to find causes and effects.

Why did Mike have obstacles when he was young? Find the causes.

1. He had a disability _____.
2. When he played as a boy, _____
   _____.
3. As a result, _____.

What is an effect of Mike refusing to accept his limitations? Tell what has happened as a result.

4. He doesn't let _____.
5. _____
6. _____

C. Think about the "Team Hoyt" passage and the passage about Mike McKeller. Decide whether each phrase shows how Mike McKeller and Rick Hoyt are similar. If a phrase shows how they are different, cross it out.

marathon races	sky diving
difficult sports	motivational speaker
disabilities	encourages people
motivated	inspiring
used a computer to communicate	parents support him
goes beyond limitations	wheelchair
adventurous as a boy	shark fishing

Name _____   Date _____

D. Write a paragraph telling why you would choose to see either Mike McKeller or Rick Hoyt in an athletic event and why this event or person is more interesting to you. Use details from the passages in your paragraph.

_____

_____

_____

_____

_____

_____

_____

_____

_____

_____

_____

_____

_____

_____

_____

_____

Name _____   Date _____

Vocabulary

"Aron Ralston: Trapped in the Canyon"

A. Write one or more numbers next to each boldfaced word to show when you have seen, heard, or used this word.

5   I use it in everyday conversation.
4   I heard it on TV or on the radio.
3   I heard or used it in school.
2   I read it in a book, magazine, or online.
1   I have not read, heard, or used this word.

☐   **solitude** (n) *being alone*
    The noisy squirrels broke the *solitude* of my morning hike.

☐   **disastrous** (adj) *causing great distress or injury*
    The rockslide was *disastrous*.

☐   **desperate** (adj) *very serious with little or no hope*
    Since no one knew where he was in the canyon, he became *desperate* to save himself.

B. Choose the word from Part A that BEST completes each sentence.

1. The _____ tornado left a path of destruction through three cities.

2. The _____ overwhelmed me when I was alone and lost in the woods.

3. In a _____ act to flee the burning house, she jumped to safety from a second-floor window.

C. Read the following definitions, then choose a synonym and an antonym from the box for each word.

| catastrophic | isolation | urgent | lucky | companionship | calm |

Words	Definitions	Synonyms	Antonyms
solitude	*being alone*		
disastrous	*causing great distress or injury*		
desperate	*serious; having little or no hope*		

Name _____   Date _____

Main Idea and Summarize

A. Complete the diagram using information from "Aron Ralston: Trapped in the Canyon."

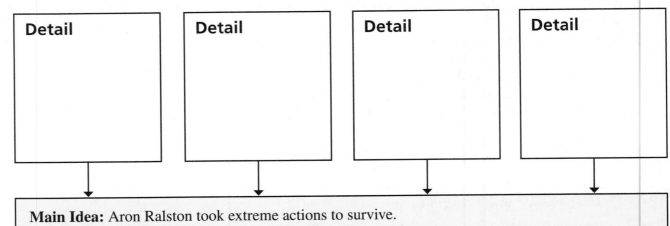

| Detail | Detail | Detail | Detail |

Main Idea: Aron Ralston took extreme actions to survive.

B. Use the main idea and supporting details to write a brief summary of "Aron Ralston: Trapped in the Canyon."

_____
_____
_____
_____
_____
_____
_____
_____
_____
_____
_____
_____
_____
_____
_____
_____
_____
_____
_____

Name _____ Date _____

Vocabulary

"Bethany Hamilton: Riding the Waves"

A. Rate your knowledge of each boldfaced word.

3   I know what this word means, and I can use it in a sentence.
2   I have an idea of this word's meaning, but I need to know more.
1   I don't know what this word means.

☐   **severed** (v) *cut off or apart*
     After her right arm was *severed*, she learned to write and eat with her left hand.

☐   **ferocious** (adj) *fierce; savage*
     The *ferocious* attack caused her to be hospitalized for a month.

☐   **impair** (v) *weaken or damage*
     She was afraid her injury would *impair* her ability to surf.

B. Read each question, then write the answer on the line.

1. Would a **ferocious** dog be wild and dangerous or friendly and gentle? _____

2. If you **severed** a rope, did you tie it in a knot or cut it in half? _____

3. If the sun could **impair** your vision, could it harm or benefit your eyes? _____

C. Some word endings, or inflections, can change the meaning of a word. The ending *-ed* changes a verb from present tense to past tense. Notice how the underlined parts of the definitions change.

Present Tense Verb		Past Tense Verb
sever *cut or slice off or apart*	+ *-ed*	**severed** *cut or sliced off or apart*
impair *weaken or damage*		**impaired** *weakened or damaged*

Choose a present or past tense verb from the charts to complete each sentence.

1. Felix's headache _____ his ability to pay attention at school that afternoon.

2. If a tree has a damaged branch, you can use a saw to _____ the branch from the trunk.

Name _____ Date _____

Compare and Contrast

Read the numbered words and phrases in the box that show ways to compare and contrast Aron Ralston and Bethany Hamilton. The numbers in the Venn diagram correspond to the topics in the box. Look at the comparison and contrast that is done for you. Then write words or phrases where they belong to complete the diagram.

1. type of accident
2. location
3. emergency help
4. how others react to them
5. what happened after injury
6. how they "gave their all"
7. obstacle
8. physical appearance
9. activity the day of accident
10. sport

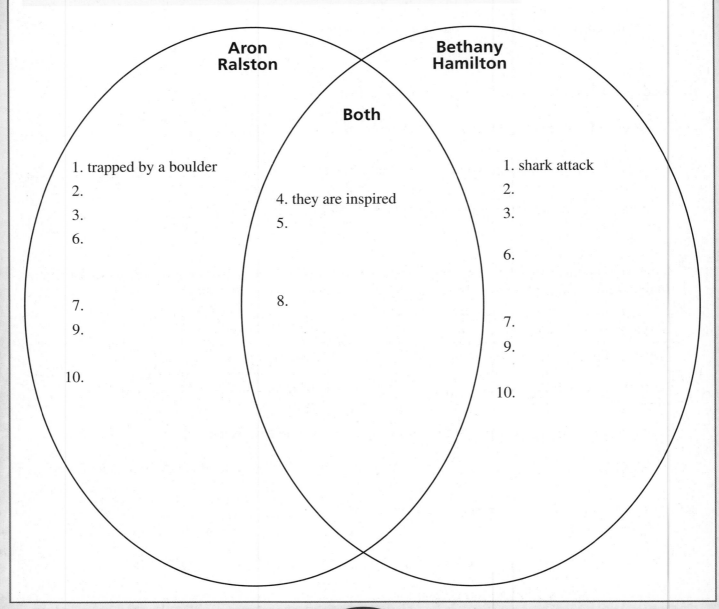

Aron Ralston

Bethany Hamilton

Both

1. trapped by a boulder
2.
3.
6.

7.
9.

10.

4. they are inspired
5.

8.

1. shark attack
2.
3.

6.

7.
9.

10.

Name _____   Date _____

Vocabulary

"9/11: Terror from the Sky"

A. Put a check mark in each row to indicate how well you know each boldfaced word.

	Know This Word	Have Seen This Word	Don't Know This Word
collapsed (v) *fell down suddenly* The towers *collapsed,* burying people under rubble.			
heroic (adj) *showing great bravery or daring like a hero* The *heroic* efforts of ordinary people saved many lives.			
gratitude (n) *feeling of being grateful for something; appreciation* The boy showed his *gratitude* for saving his dog.			

B. Read each statement. Circle true or false.

1. After a bridge **collapsed**, cars traveled over it safely.   true   false

2. A **heroic** person stands by while others save a drowning person.   true   false

3. Someone might express **gratitude** by giving flowers.   true   false

C. The Latin root *grat* means "pleasing." Many English words with *grat* relate to feeling pleased or thankful. Read the following words and meanings. Write the word that BEST completes each sentence.

congratulate	*show pleasure for an achievement*	**gratuity**	*money or a gift given for good service; tip*
ingrate	*ungrateful person*	**gratifying**	*pleasing or satisfying*

1. The diners left a _____ for the waiter.

2. Jason was angry although everyone helped him, so they said he was an _____.

3. Repairing her own car is _____ for Louisa; she feels good when it's done.

4. The principal will _____ students who entered projects in the science fair.

Name _____   Date _____

Inference

A. Read "9/11: Terror from the Sky" and complete the statements to make inferences.

What Is in the Text	What I Already Know	What I Infer
Two hijacked planes flew into the World Trade Center towers.		Terrorists wanted to
Jan Demczur escaped from an elevator with the squeegee handle.		Many objects
Rose Riso took her duty as fire warden seriously.		The people Rose worked with
Two unnamed firefighters climbed up the stairs of the north tower after the plane hit.		The firefighters

B. Use what you read and what you know to answer the questions.

What was your definition of a hero before reading "9/11: Terror from the Sky"? How did it change after you read the passage?

_____

_____

_____

Name _____   Date _____

Vocabulary

"Flight 93"

A. Rate your knowledge of each boldfaced vocabulary word.

3   familiar
2   somewhat familiar
1   unknown

> **anguish** (n) *great suffering caused by worry, grief, or pain; agony*
> We will never forget the *anguish* we experienced on September 11, 2001.

> **valor** (n) *courage or bravery*
> People will always remember the *valor* of the passengers on Flight 93.

> **confrontation** (n) *an open conflict or clashing of forces*
> The *confrontation* between the pilots and terrorists frightened the passengers.

B. Read each question, then write the answer on the line.

1. Would someone feel **anguish** by watching a car race or a car accident?

   _____

2. Would a person of **valor** receive a medal of honor or a prison sentence?

   _____

3. Would a **confrontation** be people coming together at a high school graduation or a riot?

   _____

C. Read the sentences. Write the vocabulary word from Part A that is the antonym of the underlined word.

1. People experienced terrible <u>joy</u> as they waited for news about people in the burning building.

   _____

2. The passengers who opposed the terrorists showed their <u>cowardice</u>. _____

3. The terrorists didn't expect to have a(n) <u>agreement</u> with the passengers. _____

Name _____   Date _____

Inference

A. Read "Flight 93," then read the statements in the What Is in the Text column. Complete the chart.

What Is in the Text	What I Already Know	What I Infer
Hijackers crashed Flights 11 and 175 into the World Trade Center towers. Flight 77 crashed into the Pentagon. Then hijackers took over Flight 93 and turned it to fly east.		

B. Think about "9/11: Terror from the Sky" and "Flight 93." What are two lasting effects of the events of September 11, 2001? Explain why these effects will continue.

_____

_____

_____

_____

_____

_____

_____

_____

_____

_____

_____

_____

_____

Name _____ Date _____

Review Vocabulary

A. Read the following paragraph. Replace each underlined word with the word from the box that is an antonym.

impair	solitude	valor	gratitude	confrontation	desperate

> People in towns live together as a community, not in 1. <u>companionship</u>. Teams of emergency workers are part of a community. They come to the aid of people in 2. <u>secure</u> situations. Firefighters prove their 3. <u>cowardice</u> by entering flaming buildings. Police might step into a dangerous 4. <u>agreement</u> with armed criminals. Paramedics rescue injured people quickly so that the injuries won't 5. <u>enhance</u> them for the rest of their lives. No matter what the situation, these emergency teams deserve our 6. <u>thanklessness</u> for their bravery. We need these everyday heroes in times of trouble.

1. _____   4. _____

2. _____   5. _____

3. _____   6. _____

B. Write the word from the box that BEST completes each sentence. Use the words in parentheses as clues.

disastrous	impair	severed	ferocious
desperate	collapsed	heroic	anguish

1. Mandy lived through a painful period of _____ (suffering, agony) following her family's tragic car accident.

2. The highway overpass _____ (fell down suddenly) during the earthquake.

3. When the windshield shattered, the glass _____ (cut apart) a blood vessel in Tyler's finger.

4. Kate is thankful for the _____ (showing bravery of a hero) lifeguard who saved her brother from drowning.

5. Rob needed stitches because of the _____ (fierce, savage) dog's bite.

6. It took months for us to complete the repairs to our town after the _____ (causing distress or injury) tornado hit.

Name _____   Date _____

Extend Vocabulary

A. Choose from the following suffixes to build new words. You may add more than one suffix. Write *yes* or *no* to indicate whether a spelling change is needed. The first one is done for you.

| -ation | -ion | -al | -ous | -ly |

Base Words	Suffixes	New Words	Is a spelling change needed?
confront	-ation	confrontation	no
confront			
desperate			no
desperate			yes
		disastrous	
disaster			
ferocity			
ferocious			
		valorous	

B. Complete each sentence with the BEST word from Part A.

1. The lost dog searched in _____ for food and shelter.

2. The counselor showed the two groups how to be less _____ and more understanding.

3. The family was saved from the burning house by a team of _____ firefighters.

4. Medical volunteers assisted families after the _____ hurricane.

5. My neighbors' dog _____ attacked a burglar who broke into their home.

6. The river flooded _____ and ruined many houses along its banks.

7. Juliet was angry that her friends left the party without her, but didn't want to have a _____ about it.

Name _____   Date _____

Assess Comprehension and Vocabulary

A. Read the following passage. Look for similarities and differences between this passage and other passages you have read.

> Anne Lamott once said, "There's not a hero out there that's going to save us. There's a hero inside." Lamott once needed to be saved herself. After her father died, she felt such anguish that she turned to drugs and alcohol. For years as a young woman, she dealt with the disastrous effects of substance abuse. It was like a confrontation with a powerful demon. But her talent was writing, and she managed to keep creating new articles and books. As her poverty and addiction increased, she felt her life spinning out of control. Lamott became desperate for a solution. One day, she wandered into a local church. Over the following months, she returned and became friends with many of the people there. With the support of her friends, she faced her demon. Finally, she became free of drugs and sober. Lamott's popular books are full of humor about her experiences and gratitude to the friends who stood by her.

B. Circle the letter of each correct answer.

1. Which word does NOT relate to *anguish*?
   A. agony
   B. grief
   C. encouragement
   D. suffering

2. Which word is a synonym for *disastrous*?
   A. conflicting
   B. fierce
   C. cautionary
   D. harmful

3. Which word is an antonym for *desperate*?
   A. secure
   B. hopeless
   C. anguished
   D. grateful

4. Which word does NOT go with *confrontation*?
   A. conflict
   B. avoidance
   C. oppose
   D. battle

Name _____ Date _____

5. Which word is an antonym for *gratitude*?

   A. thanklessness

   B. gratefulness

   C. recognition

   D. appreciation

6. What is the topic of this passage?

   A. topics of Anne Lamott's books

   B. how Anne Lamott overcame addiction

   C. Anne Lamott's friendships

   D. how writers can help people in poverty

7. Which sentence is the main idea of the passage?

   A. Anne Lamott used persistence and support of friends to overcome substance abuse.

   B. Anne Lamott wrote about her experiences and at last overcame drug and alcohol abuse.

   C. Writers of novels and nonfiction can overcome addiction more quickly.

   D. Anne Lamott's friends convinced her to confront her addiction, but she refused.

8. What is the reason Lamott started abusing alcohol and drugs?

   A. Alcoholism and drug addiction run in her family.

   B. She had friends who were abusing drugs and alcohol.

   C. Drugs and alcohol distracted her from her grief.

   D. Anne was bored and dissatisfied with life.

9. Which sentence from the passage contains a detail that is LEAST important to the main idea?

   A. For years as a young woman, she dealt with the disastrous effects of substance abuse.

   B. With the support of her friends, she faced her demon.

   C. Lamott became desperate for a solution.

   D. But her talent was writing, and she managed to keep creating new articles and books.

10. Which statement BEST expresses what Lamott thinks a hero is?

   A. A hero is someone famous who inspires many people.

   B. A hero is someone who overcomes personal obstacles in life.

   C. A hero is someone who sacrificed his or her own life for others.

   D. A hero is a friend who saves another friend from addiction.

11. According to the passage, what could be the reason for Lamott's poverty?

   A. Her father didn't leave her any money when he died.

   B. She published few books, and none were popular.

   C. She gave all her money to her friends who also were addicted.

   D. She spent her income on her addictions.

Name _____ **Date** _____

12. What is one way Anne Lamott and Aron Ralston are alike?

    A. A hero saved them from disaster.

    B. They were each desperate for a solution.

    C. They were both unhappy most of the time.

    D. Drugs affected their lives.

13. What MOST LIKELY would have happened if Lamott's life kept "spinning out of control"?

    A. She would become more addicted and quit writing.

    B. She would enter a hospital and continue writing.

    C. She would start a center for writers like herself.

    D. She would be unhappier but more creative as a writer.

14. What is a difference between Anne Lamott and Bethany Hamilton?

    A. only one survived a tragic injury

    B. only one has written about her experience

    C. only one encourages and inspires other people

    D. only one looked to a personal faith for help

15. Summarize Anne Lamott's struggle against substance abuse and how she overcame her problems.

_____

_____

_____

_____

_____

_____

_____

Name _____   **Date** _____

Reteach

A. Read the following passage, then answer the questions.

> Can you imagine yourself as someone who gives aid to the victims of disasters like an Asian tsunami? People in many lands welcome workers who want to work with them to make life better. Throughout the world, countries face difficulties from HIV/AIDS, poor agricultural systems, and environmental problems. The Peace Corps has become part of the solution. These workers from the United States are mostly young men and women who travel to and live for several years in communities in other countries. They may work as teachers and mentors to children and help them develop computer skills. They educate families about HIV/AIDS and family health care. They work on community projects that improve farming and water systems. What do workers gain? They may learn to speak a different language and experience a different culture. Peace Corps workers have the reward of knowing that they extended a helping hand to people who needed it.

B. Use what you already know to answer the questions.

What is a tsunami?

_____

What would be the effects of HIV/AIDS, poor agricultural systems, and environmental problems in a country?

_____

C. Find details in the passage to answer the questions.

Who usually serves in the Peace Corps? _____

_____

Name three kinds of work Peace Corps workers do. _____

_____

D. Use what you read and what you already know to make inferences.

Why would people want to join the Peace Corps?

People might want to join the Peace Corps because _____

_____.

What qualities would a Peace Corps worker need?

_____

_____

_____

Affixionary

Prefixes	Definitions	Examples
a-	on or in; to	adrift, afloat, alive, asleep
ab-	from or away	abduct, absent, abuse
ad- *(ac-, af-, ag-,* *al-, an-, ap-,* *ar-, as-, at-)*	to, toward, in, or near	address, adhere, admit, adverb
ambi-	both	ambidextrous, ambiguity
ante-	before	antebellum, antecedent
anti-	opposite or against	antibiotic, antihero, anticlimax
be-	completely, thoroughly, or excessively	befuddle, bedevil, beloved
bene-	well or good	benefit, benefactor, benevolent
circum-	around or about	circumference, circumnavigate, circumstantial
con- *(co-, col-,* *com-, cor-)*	together; with, joint, or jointly	concentrate, condemn, consider, confront
contra-	against; opposite	contradict, contraband, contrapositive
counter-	contrary; opposite	counterbalance, counterattack, counterfeit
de-	down or away from	defeat, defect, deport, deform
dis- *(dif-)*	not, absence of, or apart	disability, discount, disfigure
dys-	bad or difficult	dysfunction, dyslexic, dystrophy
ex- *(e-)*	out	export, expand, extract, expert
fore-	before	forefather, foreground, foresight
in- *(il-, im-, ir-)*	in, on, or toward	increase, infect, infer

Prefixes	Definitions	Examples
in- (il-, im-, ir-)	not	inability, inaccurate, insanity
inter-	between	interact, interchangeable, interview
intra-	within	intrapersonal, intramuscular, intrastate
intro-	in or inward	introduce, introspect, introvert
mal-	bad or badly; abnormal	maladjusted, malfunction, malpractice
mid-	middle	midline, midsection, midpoint
mis-	bad or badly; wrong or wrongly	mislead, misspell, mistake
multi-	many or much	multicolor, multiply, multivitamin
non-	not or negative	nonfat, nonsense, nonstop
ob- (oc-, of-, op-)	down, against, or facing; to	object, oblige, obsess
per-	through or completely	perfect, perform, persecute, persuade
post-	after, behind, or following	postdate, postwar, postmark
pre-	before or earlier	prearrange, preheat, premix
pro-	forward, earlier, or prior to	proclaim, profile, progress
re-	back or again	rebirth, reform, reproach, rewrite
se-	apart or aside; without	secede, seduce, separate
sub- (suc-, suf-, sug-, sup-, sus-)	under, beneath, or below; secondary	subcontract, subject, submarine, subway
syn- (syl-, sym-)	together or with	synchronize, syndrome, synthetic
trans-	across or beyond	transact, transcribe, transport, transpire
un-	to undo or reverse	unfold, unwrap, unpack
un-	not or opposite of	unable, unhappy, unwilling

Prefixes Relating to Numbers	Definitions	Examples
uni-	one	unicycle, uniform, universe
mono-	one	monologue, monopoly, monograph
bi-	two	biannual, bicycle, bipolar
duo-	two	dual, duet
di-	two	digraph, dioxide
tri-	three	triangle, tricycle, tripod
quadr-, quar-	four	quadruple, quarter, quartet
quint-	five	quintet, quintuplet
pent-	five	pentagon, pentathlon
sex-	six	sextuple, sextuplet
hex-	six	hexagon, hexameter
sept-	seven	septet, septuplet
hept-	seven	heptagon, heptameter
octa- (octo-)	eight	octagon, octopus, octuplet
nona- (nove-)	nine	nonagon
dec- (deci-, deca-)	10	decimate, decathlon, decade
cent-	100	centigrade, century
hect-	100	hectare, hectogram
milli-	1,000	millipede, millimeter
kilo-	1,000	kilogram, kilometer
myria-	10,000	myriad, myriameter
mega-	million	megabyte, megawatt
giga-	billion	gigabyte, gigahertz

Suffixes	Definitions	Parts of Speech	Examples
-able (-ible)	able; can do	(adj)	bearable, enjoyable, loveable
-ade	result of action	(n)	blockade, marinade, serenade
-age	collection; mass; relationship	(n)	baggage, drainage, wreckage
-al, -ial (-cial, -tial)	relating to or characterized by	(adj)	betrayal, internal, perennial, professional
-an (-ian)	relating to	(adj) or (n)	American, cosmopolitan, veteran
-ant	action or state	(n)	attendant, immigrant, stimulant
		(adj)	dominant, truant, vibrant
-ar	in a way	(adj)	muscular, particular, singular
-ard	one habitually in a specified condition	(n)	drunkard, coward
-ary	relation to; place where	(n)	anniversary, judiciary, vocabulary
		(adj)	cautionary, contrary, secondary
-ate	cause or make	(v)	dedicate, hesitate, radiate, ventilate
		(adj)	considerate, desolate, ultimate
-cide	kill	(n)	genocide, suicide, homicide, pesticide
-cy (-acy)	state, condition, or quality	(n)	bankruptcy, policy, accuracy, privacy
-dom	quality, realm, office, or state	(n)	boredom, freedom, stardom, wisdom
-ee	one who receives the action	(n)	absentee, employee, trustee, refugee
-eer	one associated with	(n)	engineer, mountaineer, volunteer
-en	made of or to make	(v)	blacken, deepen, enlighten, weaken
		(adj)	frozen, spoken, wooden
-ence	action, state, or quality	(n)	confidence, difference, independence
-ency	action, state, or quality	(n)	fluency, efficiency, urgency
-ent	one who; inclined to	(n)	president, patient, resident
		(adj)	diligent, intelligent
-er	one who; that which	(n)	banker, boxer, dancer, performer

Suffixes	Definitions	Parts of Speech	Examples
-ery	relating to, quality, or place where	(n)	bakery, trickery, flattery
-ese	related to	(n) or (adj)	Chinese, legalese, Portuguese
-ess	feminine	(n)	actress, hostess, princess
-ette	small	(n)	dinette, cigarette, rosette
-fold	related to a specified number or quantity	(n)	twofold, tenfold
-ful	full of or full	(adj)	armful, forgetful, shameful, wasteful
-fy, -ify	make	(v)	beautify, falsify, purify, satisfy
-hood	condition, state, or quality	(n)	boyhood, fatherhood, neighborhood, likelihood
-ian (-cian)	one having a certain skill or art	(n)	electrician, musician, statistician
-ic	of, pertaining to, or characterized by	(adj)	academic, optimistic, symbolic
-ile	relating to, suited for, or capable of	(n)	automobile, juvenile, textile
		(adj)	fertile, hostile, versatile
-ine	nature of	(n)	discipline, medicine, heroine, chlorine, vaccine
		(adj)	divine, genuine, feminine, pristine
-ing	action, process, or art	(n)	gathering, drawing
-ion (-sion, -tion)	act of, state of, or result of	(n)	admission, possession, exclusion, ambition, creation, reduction
-ish	origin, nature, or resembling	(adj)	babyish, sluggish, stylish
-ism	doctrine, system, manner, condition, act, or characteristic	(n)	capitalism, heroism, optimism, terrorism
-ist	one who	(n)	artist, cyclist, florist, optimist
-ite	nature of; quality of	(n)	favorite, parasite, satellite
-ive	causing or making	(adj)	abrasive, defensive, explosive, perceptive

Suffixes	Definitions	Parts of Speech	Examples
-ize	make	(v)	criticize, legalize, socialize
-less	without	(adj)	ageless, careless, endless, timeless
-ling	very small	(n)	duckling, kindling, yearling
-logy (-ology)	science or study of	(n)	anthology, biology, meteorology, zoology
-ly	like or manner of	(adv)	carefully, faintly, quickly, sadly
-ment	act of, state of, or a result of	(n)	agreement, engagement, movement, sentiment
-most	most or nearest to	(adj)	innermost, upmost
-ness	state of	(n)	alertness, gladness, wellness
-or	one who; that which	(n)	ancestor, editor, liberator, mediator
-ory	relating to, quality, or place where	(n)	category, history, territory
-ory	of pertaining to, or characterized by	(adj)	auditory, mandatory, sensory
-ous (-ious, -cious, -tious)	full of or having	(adj)	dangerous, generous, ridiculous, vigorous
-ship	office, state, dignity, skill, quality, or profession	(n)	censorship, membership, scholarship, township
-some	characterized by a specified quality, condition, or action	(adj)	awesome, bothersome, tiresome, wholesome
-ster	one who is associated with, participates in, makes, or does	(n)	gangster, jokester, youngster
-tude	condition, state, or quality of	(n)	altitude, gratitude, multitude, solitude
-ty, -ity	state or quality of	(n)	capacity, liberty, reality, stupidity
-ure (-ture)	state of, process, function, or office	(n)	closure, leisure, procedure, literature, torture
-ward	expressing direction	(adj)	backward, inward, onward, wayward
-y	inclined to	(adj)	brawny, cloudy, flashy, funny